ANOTHER
100 + IDEAS
FOR
DRAMA

ANOTHER
100 + IDEAS
FOR
DRAMA

Anna Scher and Charles Verrall

HEINEMANN EDUCATIONAL BOOKS
London   Portsmouth (NH)

1 33049

HEINEMANN EDUCATIONAL BOOKS LTD
22 Bedford Square, London WC1B 3HH

HEINEMANN EDUCATIONAL BOOKS INC
70 Court Street, Portsmouth, New Hampshire, 03801

LONDON   EDINBURGH   MELBOURNE   AUCKLAND
SINGAPORE   KUALA LUMPUR   NEW DELHI
IBADAN   NAIROBI   JOHANNESBURG   KINGSTON

© Anna Scher and Charles Verrall 1987
First published in 1987
Reprinted 1987

Frontispiece photo by Tony Russell

CIP Data

1. Drama in Education.   2. Improvisation (acting).
3. Children's Plays—Presentation, etc.   I. Verrall, Charles.
II. Title.   III. Title: Another one hundred plus ideas for drama.
PN3171.S275   792'.0226   86–29416

ISBN 0 435 18800 3

Typeset by Latimer Trend & Company Ltd, Plymouth
Printed and bound in Great Britain by
Richard Clay Ltd, Bungay, Suffolk

The authors at work

Contents

Acknowledgements

Sincere thanks to Christie Knipe for typing the manuscript and for her help and support and to the past and present members of the Anna Scher Theatre for their constant inspiration.

Introduction

Another 100 + Ideas for Drama is the sequel to *100 + Ideas for Drama* and like its predecessor it is intended to be used as a source book by drama teachers, students, youth and community workers, members of theatre groups – in fact by anyone who is interested in drama for or by young people. Like the previous volume it can be described as a recipe book, containing hundreds of drama ideas in improvisation which can be used in a variety of ways; but, whereas in *100 + Ideas for Drama* the emphasis was on short drama workshop exercises, here there is a greater concentration on more developed ideas that require a longer time-span, or can be extended from session to session, or can provide the theme for a whole term's work, or make a production for performance to an audience.

There are chapters on 'Developed Work in Improvisation', 'Channelling Creativity', 'Umbrella Themes', 'Short Productions' and 'Full-Scale Productions'. In each chapter the introductory paragraphs are followed by a wealth of ideas presented in a way that makes them easy to follow, use and adapt to whatever your particular situation may be – from classroom to living-room, from youth club to theatre studio. In general we have used the words 'class' and 'teacher' to represent the group and the person leading it, but that does not mean that any of the work in the book need be limited to a school setting. Neither have we been specific about the age range with which particular ideas can be used. Many of them, with suitable variations in approach, can cover the whole range from infants to adults, or large parts of it. In this, common sense and trial and error are the best guides.

The last chapter, 'More Ideas', contains additional material in all the categories used in *100 + Ideas for Drama* that we have developed in the years since that book came out. Both short and snappy ideas and solid and developed ones are included alongside one another for you to adapt to your own individual way of working. There is also a short section on video work.

WHY IMPROVISATION?

Improvisation – making it up as you go along – is the most

immediate form of drama. In an improvisation, the participants become part of the action straight away, without any lengthy preparation or memorizing. It does not demand any skills of literacy. While keeping in touch with the everyday concerns of the participants, it enables them to express deeper feelings as well. The skills it does use and develop are articulacy and the ability to be aware of and draw on one's own emotions. Expressing and understanding one's own emotions *and* those of others is an important, and neglected, area of education. The experience of having to stand in someone else's shoes and feel as he or she feels will help the individual to think through the results of his or her actions in real life. This develops tolerance, understanding and appreciation. Practice in speaking articulately and having to express oneself clearly is particularly valuable in a system in which the stress is generally on written, rather than oral, education. Imagination, again, is stimulated and developed through being used.

Because of its immediacy, improvisation is a valuable teaching tool in itself; it enables a teacher to 'get round the class' and give the maximum number of people the maximum amount of time with the maximum level of involvement. Beyond the obvious applications to social and moral education, improvisation can be applied to help teach literature, history, Greek mythology, the Bible, and so on.

Despite its accessibility, improvisation is not just 'instant theatre'. An improvisation need not be just an isolated piece of work that is produced, used and then thrown away. It can be kept, developed and built on, and this book deals particularly with the processes involved in this – the creation of developed work that has its roots in improvisation.

One thing that is of paramount importance – and this is where the role of teacher or director comes in – is to provide a clear, positive brief. Only the most highly skilled, and confident, can spin improvisations out of thin air. Start with something specific, even though things may later change, for, as King Lear said to Cordelia, 'Nothing will come of nothing'.

HOW DOES IMPROVISATION RELATE TO WORK WITH WRITTEN PLAYS?

First, always remember that the text is not the play. Plays are live events that appear on a stage; the books they are written in are, if you like, a kind of storage device. But they are essential because, without them, the unique creations of individual playwrights would not survive.

So what does experience of improvisation equip your students with when they approach a script for the first time? They should be looking on the characters as live people, existing in all their dimensions of thought and feeling. They should be looking at the way each character relates to the other characters and particularly how this changes as time elapses and we pass turning-points in the plot. Even in plays where characters are personifications of abstract qualities, they must still have their special individual human characteristics.

Because of this, when working on a specific play, improvisation can provide a particularly important stepping-stone to the text. Working from improvisation to the text and vice versa helps give the character in the play his own unique persona, his own flesh and blood and understanding. How does he or she feel in relation to the others in the play? Does he or she know how they feel about him? Through improvisation an actor can find his character.

Specific methods that can be used in rehearsal are to improvise the content (action, conflicts and emotion) of particular scenes without using the words of the playwright, or to improvise round the characters, playing scenes between them that are not in the actual play but might have happened. Characters can be interviewed and describe themselves (in character), their life and what happens to them in the play.

All this will help to flesh out and realize the characters, but you must always respect the playwright, who has created them to speak and behave in a certain way. If, through improvisation, you find a different interpretation that is going to alter this, then there must be a dramatically valid reason – and you must not diminish the strength of the play as a whole.

CLASS CONTENT

How do you go about putting together the improvisational ideas in this book to make a useful drama session or class?

First, always remember your general educational aims: to increase your students' knowledge of themselves and others, to develop their talents and to supplement the rest of their education.

Certain ground rules must be laid down at the very start. The first is: 'When you talk – I listen to you; when I talk – you listen to me.' This is simple good manners and it works both ways. It's a case of 'Do unto others as you would have them do unto you'. Students need to be told that before they can learn to act they must learn to be a good audience. Theatre is an art-form and as in all art-forms there are skills to be learnt. This requires discipline, but discipline must not be imposed in a way that stifles creativity, so it must be tempered with humour – though not at the expense of members of the class who may be more sensitive than you realize.

⚬ Suppose a newcomer is joining the class on his or her first day. After a warm welcome, allocate a special friend to look after him or her. Then firmly, but in a friendly way, establish that first ground rule of audience behaviour. Introduce the idea of improvisation, which may be a new one and, perhaps, extend this to the importance of believability, listening to one another and sharing with the audience. Sharing is an important keyword. Besides being a vital thing in itself, the use of drama ideas that involve sharing – problems, recommendations, recipes, ideas, friendships – helps students to become members of a cohesive, harmonious group. Another important way of doing this at the beginning of a session is for everyone, led by yourself, to find a space and take part in a really thorough warm-up. Follow a vigorous physical warm-up, done to music, with a verbal warm-up, such as some of the popular tongue-twisters you'll find later on in the book. After the warm-up everyone should be relaxed physically, concentrating mentally, and ready to get on with the session.

After this, use a carefully planned programme of drama workshop ideas, perhaps starting with some quickfire work that involves everybody. Then use some 'think on your feet' exercises such as 'talkabouts'. Continue with some developed work in characters, or more evolved improvisations or plays. End on a high note with an 'endgame' or something else that everyone takes part in together. After that, briefly summarize a key point that has been covered, give thanks or praise to anyone who specially merits it and remind the group when you will next be seeing them.

Always have more material prepared than you will need. That way you are covered. Be flexible; be ready to slip items into your programme or alter them as the situation demands. Be sensitive to the mood of the class so that, for example, you can put in a couple of minutes of something completely different as a light interlude to a heavy piece of work.

If you are following a theme, it can be brought in or referred to in several items in a lesson. The aim is to make an integrated, logical whole, but don't allow your sessions to become predictable. You must have an organized framework, but part of the appeal of drama should be its spontaneity. Not always knowing what is going to happen next helps to develop lively minds. So always be on the lookout for something new and, if you can at the same time build up a repertoire of old favourites that everyone likes doing, so much the better.

Every class is different, so trial and error is an essential part of the process. Be prepared to experiment, and carefully monitor the results, both as you work and afterwards. Keep a record of the ideas you use and review the situation regularly, looking back on your classroom comments on what worked and what didn't work; keeping an eye on each individual's progress, particularly those who most need encouragement.

Set aside times, say once a term, when you discuss content with the class. What do they want more of, what do they want less of, what do they want that's different? Gauge the general feeling but don't make it a popularity poll; it's your own responsibility to make the final decisions.

Finally, don't be disappointed because you can't do the perfect job; no teacher ever can. If there are setbacks learn from them; if there are successes build on them.

METHODS AND INFLUENCES

It is not only prudent but also wise to be open to all kinds of influences rather than taking a blinkered view. Don't just follow one guru. Have a pluralistic outlook. There are many different theorists in theatre and educational drama and there is something to be learned from each of them.

Stanislavsky, co-founder of the Moscow Arts Theatre, said, 'One must love art and not oneself in art' and 'All acting is giving and receiving'. He believed in a simple, truthful interpretation, and that acting was a matter of *being*, rather than doing.

Bertolt Brecht spoke about the 'alienation effect' – which has nothing to do with alienating the audience but means that audience and actors should always retain a critical distance, remaining aware that the play is not real life and that a particular message is being put across. While Stanislavsky's approach is very much to do with emotion and empathy, Brecht's is about logic and reason. Technique is emphasized. The actors must never get so carried away in the part that they lose touch with the political or social implications.

Lee Strasberg, director of the New York Actors' Studio, was the principal exponent of the Method, an American adaptation of the work of Stanislavsky, in which the actor immerses himself completely in his role. The Method uses improvisation as a training tool. It is an approach which tends to regard actors as individuals rather than members of a team and has produced such stars as James Dean and Marlon Brando.

These are theorists of the public theatre, but their ideas apply equally to drama in general and we incorporate elements from each of them in our work at the Anna Scher Theatre.

We have three golden rules: believability, listening and sharing. We passionately believe in people's individuality — but individuals working within a team. Technique starts becoming important as soon as an audience is present; as soon as people are watching, include them rather than exclude them. Technique is needed to ensure that there is no obstruction between the actor and the audience he is trying to reach.

Consideration of purposes and messages is essential as soon as you are dealing with plays. Knowledge is required both about the subject of a play and about the way human beings behave in real life.

But drama is inescapably about people's feelings and it is also an activity in which people must work together and understand the feelings of others. Seeing a situation from another point of view from one's own not only makes one a better actor but also a more tolerant and understanding person. We have an exercise in which someone sounds off on a particular subject; then the same person does the exercise from a diametrically opposed point of view — using the best points of the opposing case, not the worst. This helps to develop an awareness of what it's like to step into someone else's shoes.

Talent thrives on training together, learning from every situation and sharing with each other.

Influences can come from anywhere — from religion, myths, proverbs, philosophy, folk stories, from other teachers and from the students you are working with. A friend of our own theatre, the actor David King, philosophizes about the importance of 'the three hums' — humanity, humility and humour. A good philosophy not just for any actor, but for any human being.

So what you bring to your teaching yourself is very important. No two teachers can be, or should be, alike. You will have things to offer that no one else has.

In life's perpetual see-saw of give and take, if you give a little more you'll usually get it back. Thus the children of today will be the good parents of tomorrow. Always encourage a generous spirit.

1

Developed Work in Improvisation

We have already discussed the value of improvisation. The requirement to use one's own words builds up articulacy and general competence in language. Both creating and producing a piece of drama, at the same time, is a powerful piece of self-expression which helps to build up self-confidence. The need to follow through consequences in a logical way is a good thinking exercise. The need to interact with other people in an improvisation develops the ability to co-operate. The need to think carefully about more than one character's thoughts and feelings in the context of the play makes a person more socially aware of those around him or her in the context of life.

This chapter is about how work in improvisation can be developed into something that is more than just 'instant theatre'.

All improvisations have to start from something. Hence the importance of a clear brief for a particular piece of work. The teacher must start off the class with instructions that are simple, concise and unambiguous. There should not be any mystique about drama; a straightforward, common-sense approach is much better. You can demystify theatre without taking away any of the magic.

Once the class have got the message, they're away. They can all work at once, and then you can spotlight particular individuals, pairs or groups for everyone to see, or you can see them one by one. With practice they'll very quickly feel the shape of an improvisation; but if a scene goes on and on the teacher can quietly interject 'Ten seconds to finish' (or twenty seconds or one minute, or whatever). This is a most useful stopping device. 'Action' and 'cut' are also useful words for beginning and ending an improvisation.

What if, having set up the 'rules of the game' for a piece of work, you find that the rules are being broken, in other words that someone is not following the brief? Generally, let it run. A good piece of work is a good piece of work even if it's not what you intended to happen. After it's over you can, if necessary, put things back on course with a comment like 'very good, but it's not what I asked for' and a reminder of the initial brief. Of course there is a difference between someone forgetting, or misunderstanding, the brief and someone who is being self-indulgent or won't accept the discipline that's necessary to work with other people; *that* you need to deal with straight away.

Sometimes an idea falls flat on its face. The class's imagination is not fired or they can't get the hang of what you mean. You have to decide then whether the brief you gave wasn't clear enough, or whether the idea is pitched at the wrong level for the class you are working with, or whether the idea itself does not provide good dramatic material, and act accordingly by altering the brief or discarding the idea altogether and moving on to something else. Generally, to stimulate good improvisation, an idea has to have the seeds of conflict, or dramatic tension, in it, whether the conflict is of an obvious or a subtle kind.

Your own preparation is important. Apart from having a programme worked out for the class, you need to have thought things through and have one or two alternatives ready in the back of your mind depending on what response you get. If you are doing work that requires a factual background, do the necessary research; it's worth re-reading things even if you already know them, just so as to have all the facts at your fingertips.

Don't flog an idea to death: no one wants to see twenty similar interpretations of the same thing, one after the other. If you want to show the class a few people's work, use your observation to spot the person who has got something good to contribute, or ask for a volunteer who's done something different. Be aware of who might benefit from an opportunity, and always be ready for people to catch your eye.

Usually, after you've given the brief, the class can start improvising straight away. For a more complex idea they may need to consult each other and decide what they're going to do before actually doing it. (During the discussion time you or your stage managers can set up for the improvisation.) At other times you may want to discuss an idea with the whole class.

While some discussion beforehand is good, don't take the steam out of an idea by discussing it for too long – leave something to the imagination. For 'Tonight We Improvise'.

Once the class has come to grips with improvising simple situations, character and plot development will gradually start to take place. Paying attention to detail – dotting the i's and crossing the t's – will begin to matter. The details of the way characters behave tell us so much about them. Technique plays an important part, as does emotion – but in the end believability is paramount. Did you really believe in the work or was it, perhaps, a shade unsubtle? Tell the class never to underestimate the intelligence of the audience. For example, elderly people are not necessarily decrepit. Encourage your class to develop more complex and interesting characters. Real people are not one-dimensional; they have their good and bad sides, their ambiguities and subtleties. And as real people change under the influences of real life, so it is one of the essentials of drama that characters should be changed by events.

Plot development progresses in the same way. At every point of an improvisation there are dozens of possibilities. Applaud a piece of work that doesn't follow the obvious path downhill but has an unexpected twist. By avoiding the predictable you can catch the audience with their guard down and make a piece more effective. Encourage your group to be sensitive to shape – beginnings, middles and ends. A circular construction, when the end is an echo of the beginning, is very satisfying. Foster an appreciation of pace – how fast things happen, pauses – the vital spaces between the words or actions – and timing – the speed of response to what the other person has said.

With a clear brief, sound groundwork, constant encouragement and constructive comment, work in improvisation will start developing well. Great oaks from little acorns grow.

ROLE REVERSAL

Role reversal is a useful and effective way of bringing the message home when it comes to seeing an opposite point of view. It is also a piece of character work in which students learn to put themselves inside the mind of someone quite different from themselves. Here are some ideas, as they might be introduced to a class. Your actors can first play the parts one way and then reverse the roles; this gives them the opportunity to experience the situation from both points of view.

Late Home from School

'Dionne, you are a single parent. Kelda is the daughter you are bringing up on your own. On this particular afternoon it's six o'clock, and Kelda is usually back from school at a quarter past four, give or take five minutes. You are worried. You've rung her best friend, Ann. You've rung the school but neither Ann nor the school know where Kelda is. You are actually on the point of ringing the police when

Kelda walks in. Your first line is "Where on earth have you been? I've been worried sick about you." What happens then? What reason is given for being late? Is it the truth? Action!'

No Application

'Tracey, you are Darren's teacher and he's been in your class for two months. Now the thing about Darren is that he has enormous talent – but he's not doing anything with it. He's just wasting time day in and day out. You say to him, "Darren, you've got talent – but no application." Action!'

Babysitter

'Dawn, you are babysitting for your sister Marcia's baby and you've done it countless times before and always done it well. On this particular occasion, however, your friend Zoe across the road asks you to come over and listen to her latest Spandau Ballet record. You'll only be two or three minutes and the baby's fast asleep anyway. You go, and just after you've gone Marcia returns and is devastated to find baby Wayne left on his own. Dawn re-enters. Marcia: "Have you gone out of your mind leaving an eight-month-old baby here on his own?" Action!'

Appearance Counts!

'Sadie, you are the manageress of a rather smart ladies' dress shop – not quite a trendy boutique but a rather upmarket place for the mature woman. Sally has been in your employment now for two weeks. You originally employed her as her references showed her to be punctual, reliable, conscientious and honest – though it has to be said that you were not impressed by her appearance, but she did make an effort on the interview. However, Sally's appearance has got steadily worse. The time has come for her to smarten up – or else. First line – "Sally, could I have a word with you?" Action!'

There are many monologue and duologue pieces in Chapter 6 that are suitable for role reversal and in the case of the monologue it's always interesting to hear the imaginary person's right of reply.

SOLILOQUIES

The soliloquy: one actor on his own speaking his thoughts to the audience. The soliloquy provides a good opportunity for an actor to get to grips with a character. By expressing his thoughts to us he is revealing the character's innermost self. We, the audience, share his thoughts and get to know him from the inside. It's an artificial device that can be made to seem entirely natural.

Take the characters from a duologue and straight after their scene tell the actors you now want to see soliloquies – at the point of time when the scene ends. So now both sides of the story are summed up clearly and without ambiguity. The soliloquy is a way of increasing self-knowledge, and it is a sharing experience.

THE IN-DEPTH INTERVIEW

Another way of finding out about characters is to ask them about themselves and have them reply *in character*. This was described in *100+ Ideas for Drama* as 'People Meet People', which is a television interview idea. To probe a little further, one can set up a situation in which a character is interviewed in depth by yourself as a psychiatrist or counsellor. This idea was inspired by Dr Anthony Clare's excellent radio series *In the Psychiatrist's Chair*, in which he interviewed a number of well-known people about the influences and relationships which had formed their lives.

Take a character from a play the class is working on, or from an improvisation, and set up a situation in which such an in-depth interview might credibly take place. For example, you could have a rebellious teenager in conversation with a friendly teacher. Help the person find his or her character by asking some routine questions such as name, age, occupation and hobbies, and then go on to ask about family background, early childhood, life history, and hopes and fears for the future. How does the subject get on with the other people in his life? How does he feel about the other characters? How does he think the other characters feel about him? What turning-points have there been?

Concentration and a sympathetic atmosphere are essential. Once in character the person has to react automatically. There's no time to think it out. Equally, the 'psychiatrist' must believe in the situation and use all his or her knowledge of human nature and psychology to draw out the key points.

Some sample questions:

'What is your earliest memory?'
'What sort of a child were you, when you were little?'

5

'Did you feel that one or other of your parents favoured you over your brothers or sisters?'

'Have you ever had a serious illness? What was it like?'

'What was the happiest time of your life?'

'What sort of person did you think your husband or wife was when you first met?'

'Was there ever a time when you began to think that life might not turn out as well as you hoped it would?'

Not only is this an effective way of developing characters, but it will also provide insights for both the class and yourself on the similarities and differences in the way people think and feel. Encourage them to observe people – how they sit, stand and walk, for example, and the way all the parts contribute to the whole person.

RELATED IMPROVISATION (OR PLAYLETS)

The 'related impro' is like a mini-play and is very effective for a school assembly piece. Each related impro is made up of three or four (usually four) separate scenes with a *vox pop* ending in which each character sums up in a line or two his or her feelings about what has happened. The teacher casts it, gives an outline of the characters and plot and uses either incidental music or maracas as a scene divider.

The Bully

> *Characters*   in order of appearance, Bully, Boy, Best Friend, Teacher
> *Set*   school playground
> *Scene 1*   Bully and Boy
> *Scene 2*   Boy and Best Friend
> *Scene 3*   Boy and Teacher
> *Scene 4*   Boy, Teacher and Bully

'Nobody likes a bully and, casting completely against type, Darren would you play the part of the bully, please? *Scene 1*: You are in the playground and you start jibing at Bernard. Bernard, you can't stand it. "Why are you always picking on me?" you say. And the scene builds up to a climax. *Scene 2*: Bernard is very upset and his best friend Mmoloki comes along. Mmoloki tries to console Bernard but this time Bernard seems to have taken it really badly. Mmoloki advises him to tell the teacher. *Scene 3*: We see the teacher, Miss

Hanson, and Bernard in conversation. Miss Hanson gives Bernard some sound advice. *Scene 4*: Bernard, Miss Hanson and Darren – are we going to see a grand reconciliation? That is up to you. As usual we end with the *vox pop.*'

No Smoking

> *Characters*   in order of appearance, Mum, Child, Aunt
> *Set*   home scene (settee, with chairs at either side, television with flowers and telephone on top)
> *Scene 1*   Mum and Child
> *Scene 2*   Child and Aunt
> *Scene 3*   Mum, Aunt and Child

'They say that smoking can be bad for your health. Heather, you are very worried about your mum. Mrs Page is now up to forty a day – ever since Dad left home. It seems clear to you, Heather, that, as every advertisement says, "cigarettes can seriously damage your health", and you are concerned that your mum seems oblivious to these warnings. You've noticed that her smoker's cough has got a lot worse over the last couple of months. You decide on a heart to heart. *Scene 1*: Mum and daughter. First line from Heather – "Mum, why don't you give up smoking?" The duologue ends with Mum having to go to her evening class. *Scene 2*: Aunt Joanne pops round and Heather confides her anxiety to her aunt (her mum's sister). Heather really is very worried. Aunt Joanne promises to have a good talk with her sister when she returns from evening class. Heather is relieved. *Scene 3*: Mum returns and is somewhat surprised to see her sister Joanne there so late. "Is anything the matter?" she says. The conversation gets a bit heavy and Heather is told by her mother to go to bed. The two sisters have an argument about Mum's smoking, the effect on her health, and the effect on Heather. *Vox pop.*'

The Tubby Child

> *Characters*   in order of appearance, School Doctor, Mum, Child, Dad
> *Set*   medical room at school and home scene
> *Scene 1*   School Doctor, Mum and Child
> *Scene 2*   Mum and Child
> *Scene 3*   Mum and Dad
> *Scene 4*   Dad and Child

'*Scene 1* is set in the medical room at school. Behind the desk is Dr Saul. In front of the doctor's desk are Sylvia and her Mum – Mrs Lewis. The prognosis is that Sylvia will have to go on a diet. She's been eating far too many sweets, sticky buns and junk foods that are bad for her. First line from the doctor: "I'm afraid, Mrs Lewis, that Sylvia will have to go on a rather strict diet." *Scene 2*: We see Mrs Lewis and Sylvia in their sitting-room. First line from Sylvia: "I want something to eat." Second line from Mrs Lewis: "You heard what the doctor said." The two of you have quite a row which culminates in Sylvia going out and slamming the door. *Scene 3*: Enter Dad – "What's the matter with you, love? You've got a face as long as Oxford Street." Mum and Dad discuss the problem of their overweight child. They decide that Dad should have a word. *Scene 4*: Dad and Sylvia. Dad – "I'd like a word with you, love." At the end of *Scene 4* we see all four characters in a *vox pop.*'

A Child's Stay in Hospital

> *Characters*   in order of appearance, Child, Mum, Nurse
> *Set*   in hospital
> *Scene 1*   Child and Mum
> *Scene 2*   Mum and Nurse
> *Scene 3*   Nurse and Child
> *Scene 4*   Mum and Child

'Most of us at some point in our lives have a short or long stay in hospital. Mark, you are in hospital for the very first time – to have your tonsils out. More than likely, you're only going to be there for a few days. *Scene 1*: We see Mark sitting up in bed reading, and bang on two o'clock, the start of visiting time, in comes his mum. First line from Mum – "How are you today, son?" Now, Mark, in fact you are fine but you play up a bit to your mum. Which is very naughty! *Scene 2*: Mum is worried – though unnecessarily – and before she goes she has a word with the nurse. Mum says, "I'm rather worried about Mark." The nurse is a very considerate lady and tells Mark's mum she has nothing to be worried about. *Scene 3*: The nurse gives a jolly good telling off to Mark. She tells him to stop playing his mum up. *Scene 4*: The next day. Mark makes it up to his mum, admitting he was exaggerating how ill he was. He genuinely apologizes. We end, as usual, with the *vox pop.*'

Divided Loyalties

> *Characters*   in order of appearance, Mum, Child, Dad, Best
>   Friend
> *Set*   home scene plus playground in school
> *Scene 1*   Mum and Child
> *Scene 2*   Mum and Dad
> *Scene 3*   Dad and Child
> *Scene 4*   Child and Best Friend

'I don't know if you've ever been in a situation where your loyalties have been divided and you're left with very mixed feelings. This is such a situation. Richard, your best friend is Billy Chatt (Sid, will you be Billy Chatt?). Now Billy Chatt's reputation is notorious. He plays knock-down-ginger on all the old ladies in Barnsbury Street – he thinks it's very smart to knock on doors and run away. He bunks off school. He gives cheek to his mum. But you, Richard, think that Billy Chatt is the bee's knees. On the other hand, your parents cannot tolerate him. They say, "Tell me who your friends are and I'll tell you who you are," but you, Richard, hotly defend Billy Chatt. *Scene 1*: Mum is just finishing a telephone call to Mrs Smithers, one of the old ladies down Barnsbury Street. Apparently Richard and Billy Chatt have been at it again – playing knock-down-ginger. Enter Richard as Mum puts the phone down. Mum – "I've had it up to here with you. Ever since you've been hanging round with that Billy Chatt." Mother and son have an almighty row which culminates in Richard being sent to his room. *Scene 2*: Dad gets back from work and both parents discuss the problem. Mum tells Dad to deal with it. She feels there's nothing more that she can do. *Scene 3*: Dad and Richard. Dad wants Richard to drop Billy Chatt. Richard's loyalties are really tested now. . . . *Scene 4*: The next day Richard has a heart-to-heart with Billy Chatt. I'll leave it to you, Richard, as to how you want to handle things. And we'll end with the *vox pop*.'

'When People Complain of Boredom
They Have Usually Done Nothing to Deserve It'

> *Characters*   in order of appearance, Mum, Child, Dad
> *Set*   home scene
> *Scene 1*   Mum and Child
> *Scene 2*   Mum and Dad
> *Scene 3*   Child, Mum and Dad

'I'd like this related impro to be topped and tailed with this saying –

"When people complain of boredom
they have usually done nothing to deserve it"

– so will you announce the title at the beginning *and* end, Martha, please? Three characters: Mum, Dad and Child. You be the child, Michael, and Dawn and Robert the mum and dad. *Scene 1*: Michael comes home from school and the first thing he does after switching on the television is say, "I'm bored." Mum, you say, "That word is not allowed in this house." *Scene 1* ends with Mum getting so exasperated with Michael that she sends him to his room. *Scene 2*: Dad returns from work. Mum and Dad have words about Michael and how he's always so bored with everything. Dad suddenly hits upon it. *He removes the television!* No more instant entertainment. Michael will have to make his own entertainment from now on. Exit Mum and Dad. *Scene 3*: Michael enters and goes to where the television would normally be. He gives a double take. Where is it? Re-enter the parents and we see what happens. I wonder if Michael has learnt any lessons! *Vox pop* – and Martha tails the scene with:

"When people complain of boredom
they have usually done *nothing* to deserve it."'

The Practical Joke that Misfired

Characters   in order of appearance, Sister, Brother, Mum
Set   home scene
Scene 1   Sister and Brother
Scene 2   Mum and Sister
Scene 3   Mum and Brother
Scene 4   Mum, Sister and Brother

'Being at the receiving end of a practical joke isn't always funny and it certainly isn't when it misfires. John and Kelda, you are brother and sister and on this particular occasion Kelda returns from school, takes off her coat and settles down to watch *Dramarama*. John, you creep up behind her wearing a grotesque mask; you put your hand on her shoulder. Kelda turns round and screams blue murder. It wasn't so much the mask that frightened her – though it is pretty grotesque – but it was all totally *unexpected*. Kelda says, "You frightened the living daylights out of me." And such is her state of shock that she proceeds to rant and rave at John. The scene ends with her in tears and you, John, cross with her for getting in such a state. You might tell her how cowardly she is. Anyway, you leave her to it and go to your room. That's *Scene 1*. *Scene 2*: Enter Mum, who is concerned to see Kelda in such distress. Kelda tells her what happened. Mum soothes her daughter and suggests that Kelda go to the kitchen (off) to make some tea. *Scene 3*: Mum calls John down and reprimands him. It transpires that no harm was meant but clearly an apology is in order. *Scene 4*: Mum with Kelda and John. John apologizes to Kelda magnanimously. He is sorry for what he has done. *Vox pop.*'

Mutton Dressed as Lamb

> *Characters* in order of appearance, Daughter, Mum, Dad
> *Set* home scene
> *Scene 1* Daughter and Mother
> *Scene 2* Mother and Father
> *Scene 3* Mother and Daughter

'When the mature woman dresses very young some people might unkindly say: "Mutton dressed as lamb". That is our situation today. Sharon and Dionne are mother and daughter and, Sharon, you're ever so proud of your mum but you feel she's been dressing a bit *too* fashionably lately. You honestly think she's past wearing the clothes that people of your age wear. Sharon, your intentions are good. You really do mean well. You simply do not want your mum to be the laughing-stock of the estate. So, in *Scene 1*, daughter Sharon has a heart-to-heart with mother Dionne about it. As to how you take it, Dionne – well, I'll leave that up to you! Sharon has certainly given her mum something to think about. *Scene 2*: Later that evening – Sharon has gone to the pictures and Dionne is watching television with her husband, Tony. Dionne, you come straight to the point: "Tony, do you think I look like mutton dressed as lamb?" Tony, I trust you'll make *sensitivity* the keynote of this scene. I'd like you to play it extremely sympathetically, listening intently, but, Dionne, I want it to be *you* that reaches your own conclusions. *Scene 3*: The next day. Mother and daughter again. It will be interesting to see what has transpired. First line from Dionne: "Sharon, I've been thinking over what you were saying to me yesterday. . . ." After *Scene 3* we'll go straight into *vox pop.*'

Lies

>   *Characters*   in order of appearance, Girl, Boy, Pick-Up Girl,
>   Jealous Friend
>   *Set*   home scene and at the bus-stop
>   *Scene 1*   Girl and Boy
>   *Scene 2*   Boy and Pick-Up Girl
>   *Scene 3*   Girl and Jealous Friend
>   *Scene 4*   Boy and Girl

'They say it's a sin to tell a lie. Well, that may be, but as far as I'm
concerned honesty is not just the best policy – it's the only policy.
Lies – black or white or fibs or sins or whatever you call them – can
only cause unhappiness. Bernard and Susan have been going out
together for three months or so but things are getting a little shaky.
It's not that Bernard isn't fond of Susan but there are other fish in the
sea and he is only sixteen. Susan is getting a touch paranoid about
Bernard and she's hearing half-truths here and there, and now from a
so-called reliable source she hears he's been seeing someone else. Has
he? We don't know. *Scene 1*: Bernard calls for Susan at her house to
be greeted by Susan saying, "You lied to me!" Bernard soon flies into
a rage himself and the scene ends with both of them flying off the
handle. Bernard leaves Sue – in a stew. *Scene 2*: At the bus-stop.
Bernard meets an old flame and proceeds to pick her up. They are
being watched by someone (the jealous friend) whom we do not see.
Scene 3: The jealous friend calls round to Susan and reports on what
she has just seen. She starts by saying "I feel sorry for you" to poor
unfortunate Sue. *Scene 4*: Bernard returns to Susan. Will they make up
or finally break up?

>   "O, what a tangled web we weave,
>   When first we practise to deceive!"

Certainly deceits and lies have no place in any relationship. I'll
leave the ending up to you. And finally the *vox pop*.'

Temptation

>   *Characters*   in order of appearance, Younger Sister, Boyfriend,
>   Older Sister
>   *Set*   home scene
>   *Scene 1*   Younger Sister and Older Sister's Boyfriend

Scene 2   Two Sisters
Scene 3   Older Sister and her Boyfriend

'Since time immemorial, when the serpent tempted Eve with the apple, temptation has reared its head again and again. Kerryann, you are Bernadette's younger sister. Costas is Bernadette's boyfriend. You're practically engaged – but not quite. *Scene 1*: Kerryann has just got back from boarding-school and Costas calls for Bernie. Bernie is at the hairdresser's. Costas can't quite conceal how grown-up and attractive Bernie's baby sister has become to him and can't resist making a pass at her. Whether things develop further is up to the two of you. Kerryann, do you find your sister's boyfriend attracrive? Are you horrified at his advances? Or flattered? And what about your loyalty to Bernie? First line from Costas: "Gosh you've changed since I last saw you!" *Scene 2*: Ten minutes later. Bernadette arrives home. Costas has gone now. We see the two sisters together. Kerryann: "Costas has just been. . . ." But something about her tone of voice makes Bernadette suspicious. How you play it largely depends on what has happened in *Scene 1*. *Scene 3*: Bernadette and Costas. I wonder if we'll see a show-down in the grand manner or not? An open scenario – it's up to you. Plus *vox pop* at the end.'

Variations

As in 'Temptation' above, you can suggest different plot alternatives to choose from, or else you can outline a related improvisation up to the point at which you give the participants a free choice of ending. You can always explore more than one variation by repeating an improvisation, directing the actors to keep as close as possible to the original until they come to the 'fork in the road', and then to take the other path. So, for example, in 'Temptation', if, the first time round, Kerryann has admitted her infatuation for Costas, the second time she can be asked to disguise it. Other variations can be created by throwing in an extra plot factor in the background – 'Costas had a terrible row with Bernie last night' – or some alteration in the personality of one of the characters – 'Kerryann is a compulsive liar'. The variations can be technical as well as in the plot or characters – 'the emotions are still there but I want you to underplay them' – or you can ask for a change of pace or style. These are not just acting exercises; they also teach something about human nature.

THE RULES OF THE GAME

This is an advanced and open-ended improvisation idea, in which an overall situation is laid down and the members of the group invent characters and perform an improvised play in which their entrances and exits are determined by a series of prearranged rules. For example:

The Mish

The Mish (short for Mission) is an inner-city youth project. The members of the group can choose any character that might appear there in an evening: teenagers of all ages and sorts – at school, at college, at work, unemployed – youth workers, voluntary helpers, teachers, neighbours, the police, and any of their family or friends. Suggest an outline in which one or more disturbed youths join the Mish and try to take it over. Float the idea that the various loyalties and emotional entanglements within the group will emerge in the story.

The rules of the game are that not more than three people can appear in the play at the same time. When one of them exits he or she unobtrusively touches someone else on the shoulder and this licenses that character to go on – though he doesn't have to go on straight away. Point out that the choice of who goes on next is vitally important as it often affects the plot and the shape of the piece. Each character is allowed to go on twice, and it is convenient if after their second exit the participants go and sit in another part of the audience, in order not to be chosen again.

Having introduced the idea and explained the rules, arrange a general-purpose set to represent a side-room at the Mish. Meanwhile the group has a chance to form their characters and find their relationships – boy- and girl-friends, sworn enemies, and so on. When they're ready, repeat the rules, and then ask the characters to introduce themselves individually, giving their name and role (for example, occupation, relationship to other characters). It's a good idea for people to retain their own names in this particular piece of work unless they need to change them for character reasons. Having heard these, designate the first three characters that are allowed to go on and, if all goes well, the play will then proceed from beginning to end.

At the first try you may need to intervene from time to time to keep things running smoothly. In your initial direction point out that the play must have a good ending and that it is up to the last three participants to find one. It is a demanding exercise, because you are asking your actors to create a coherent plot, as they go, within an arbitrary structure. Selfish acting will kill the whole thing, and too many high dramatic moments will make it farcical, but if the actors are sensitive to each other and pick up on references from within the story a satisfactory play will emerge.

The rules for 'The Mish' would suit a group of a dozen or so but there is room for any amount of variation to suit the number of people, the length of time and the storyline you have chosen. For example, you can allow more people on stage at once (though too large a number quickly get out of control); you can allow each character a normal ration of only one appearance, unless specially chosen to reappear by one of the other actors; you can make one character a 'wild card' who can come or go as he or she pleases; you can use music to dissolve a scene and signal the passage of time, in which case the next scene begins with a new set of characters; or you can say that there will be a series of scenes in different places and draw names out of a hat to determine who appears in each scene — some, of course, more than once.

Other suggested situations:

The Pop-Inn   A fast-food restaurant one lunch time. The characters are the staff (permanent and temporary) and the customers — people having their lunch break, shoppers, people who've arranged to meet or who meet by accident.

Neighbours   The Swears, a very coarse family, live between the Upneys, a social-climbing family, and the Priests, a narrow, religious family. It is a hot day and the action takes place in and out of their back gardens. Suggest some situations — for example, young Miss Upney is sunbathing and young Mr Priest decides to convert her; the Swears' dog is about to mate with the Upneys' pedigree poodle, etc.

Tourists Stranded   Flights home from Santa Paloma have been postponed indefinitely so a party of tourists is stranded. The set can be the hotel lobby, poolside and a bedroom (to represent anyone's bedroom). The characters are the tourists (all ages, some in families or couples), the Santa Paloman hotel staff, tourists from other countries, and so on.

Warren Drive   A prosperous suburb. Most of the husbands are out all day, but the wives are at home. Sometimes they visit their neighbours. There are some children and teenagers. There are milkmen, decorators, plumbers, meter-readers, and anyone who's on the end of a telephone. All manner of domestic dramas may take place.

Plato Park   A television soap opera that's been on for twenty years. There is the regular cast among whom many relationships, good and bad, have developed. There are the actors in the smaller parts, the producer who created the series, the new director and possibly some of the crew. It is the lunch break during filming. Perhaps the characters should be asked when introducing themselves to say what they *really* feel about the programme.

The Ark   A group of people live communally in a remote country house because they believe that civilization is about to end. They believe in the development of 'inner space' through meditation, etc., and in 'absolute truth' – unwelcome facts must not be concealed. Two of the group are designated as leaders, and two more as newcomers; the rest are members of the commune.

Linda and Perry   Each person has a relationship – love or friendship – with two other people, either concurrently or consecutively. The first scene is played between A and B; the surroundings can be whatever they like. After this scene A chooses C, who will be B's next partner in a different scene in fresh surroundings. And so the chain continues until A reappears in the last scene.

Heroes in Paradise   This is set in the place where heroes go when they die. They may be famous people, heroes of fiction, or invented heroes, but here they spend eternity remembering their past triumphs, discussing the meaning of existence, and living together in the everlasting present. The characters introduce themselves by announcing their name and showing us a 'clip' of their earthly existence, which typifies them. One or two may be new arrivals.

THREES, GROUPS AND CROWD SCENES

As soon as there are more than two actors working together an important rule is that they don't all talk at once. They need to act in a *giving* way; if they are too 'busy', you will get a spiral effect in which people will try to top one another in order to grab the audience's attention. Listening, as always, is of the essence. And of course the greater the number, the greater the importance of having a clear, specific brief.

The Eternal Triangle

'Gillian and Oona, you share a flat together. Oona's boy-friend is

Tony; you've been going out together for a year. Every Tuesday Oona goes to an evening class at the local arts centre, but on this particular evening it's been cancelled and she comes back early to find her boyfriend, Tony, in the arms of her flatmate, Gillian.

'Can we start inside the flat, at the point half a minute *before* Oona returns.'

The teacher might ask for a soliloquy from each of the characters after the scene.

Spoilt for Choice

Take three boys – Sid, John and Wayne. It's a Saturday afternoon. Sid wants to go to the Michael Sobell Sports Centre, John wants to go to the Arsenal and Wayne wants to go to the Screen on the Green to see the latest Eddie Murphy film. Maybe Sid uses a bit of friendly persuasion on the others. Maybe John and Wayne agree to go to the Arsenal and Sid goes off on his own. Or maybe you all three go your separate ways and meet up later. Can you reach a happy compromise?'

The Intermediary

'I want the whole class to go into threes. The threes can be made up of family, friends or acquaintances. They might be mum, dad and daughter. Or three girl friends. Or employer and two employees. Whatever. The point is that two of the three are in conflict and the other acts as the intermediary. Can the intermediary, or go-between, bring the conflicting pair to harmony? Or at least can we fall back on that good old British compromise? Or are they going to stay in conflict?'

Two's Company, Three's a Crowd

'The home scene, please. I want Tracey and her boy-friend Mark watching *Top of the Pops* cosily on the sofa. Tracey's parents have gone to Margate for the week. The only thing to mar Tracey's joy is that she has to mind Joanna, her younger sister, who is mischief personified. It's a definite case of "Two's company, three's a crowd".'

Here are some firm favourites for *group work*.

Locations and Incidents

Each group chooses a location – the launderette, school, court, heaven, hell, the hairdresser's, the dentist's waiting-room, adventure

playground, gymnasium, prison cell – wherever. An incident occurs at
the location: perhaps at the launderette the washing machine
overflows; perhaps at the adventure playground someone finds a bag
containing £2,000 in used fivers. Whatever it is, something happens!
We see the lead–up, the incident and the aftermath.

Chain Argument

Person No. 1 is minding his own business. Enter Person No. 2, who
picks an argument with No. 1 – 'Where's the £5 I lent you last
week?' The argument develops and culminates in No. 1 leaving. Enter
No. 3, who now picks a different argument with No. 2 until No. 2
exits. Enter No. 4 – and so on. Go on until the first person comes
back again to complete the chain – No. 1 arguing with No. 8.
Listening is of paramount importance as references from previous
arguments can perhaps be brought into later ones. A variation is to
have the chain argument in whispers.

The Rumour

The structure of this is similar to the 'Chain Argument' but with a
touch of 'Chinese Whispers'. Two people start off a rumour. You can
give them a first line – 'Did you hear that Jenny's been sacked from
her Saturday job?' After that duologue, one of them exits and the
other repeats the rumour to a new person, somewhat changing the
facts. The third picks up with a fourth, the fourth with a fifth, and so
on till the rumour grows out of all proportion. In the end it gets back
to the first person again. Tell them not to make the changes too
unsubtle – just a little exaggeration goes a long way!

Family Occasions

All families have their ups and downs. Take a family occasion –
sister's twenty-first, cousin's wedding, grandma's seventieth birthday,
Christmas dinner, a baby's christening, a great uncle's funeral.
Whether it is a time for celebration or for commiseration, the object
of the exercise is for something to happen which changes the flavour
of the occasion. For example, as the turkey is being carved a daughter
announces that she has turned vegetarian.

Divide the class into groups of from four to six, appoint leaders
and give them a few minutes preparation time.

Group Gossips

Women are supposed to gossip much more than men. But do they? Have a group of women gossips, a group of men gossips and a mixed group. Choose a location – mothers waiting for their children outside the school gates, the men's changing room of a sports club, the bar of a social club. A good first line – 'Have you heard the latest?'

Table Talk

Group people round tables in a restaurant. Conversations start round each table. The teacher 'freezes' them, then spotlights each table in turn, in no particular order, 'actioning' and 'cutting' them. After each 'cut' the group freezes till the teacher 'actions' them again. To warm them up each member of the group can order a meal from the menu – in character, of course. The teacher can be the waitress or waiter taking the orders. Then the table talk commences.

You can add to the brief if you like by designating various characters, such as a four-year-old or an American cousin; or groups, such as a family party, a business meal, or a staff outing; or plot points – perhaps one person must be given a very bad piece of news. Warn them not to be too 'busy'.

In this, as in many other exercises, the teacher can have a director's role in shaping the idea as it progresses, by choosing which table to cut to next, and putting in a word about what may have been happening in the interim, so that the whole piece will have a beginning, a middle and an end.

Teacher and Pupils

This is an exercise which must *not* be sent up. Each group has a teacher and the rest of the group are pupils. The teacher takes a class in whatever subject he or she chooses, for example, a geography lesson on Ireland, how to make an omelette, a computer studies lesson on programming. The teacher delivers an introduction and takes it to the point where the pupils are set to work by themselves.

This is a very good exercise for characterization and teamwork but you must emphasize the importance of keeping the teacher characters realistic rather than stereotyped, and the pupils must resist the temptation to get out of control. Another believability point is that the content of the teachers' lessons has to be accurate – they can't get away with waffling any more than a real teacher can!

Winning and Losing

Perhaps you can learn more from losing than from winning. Have a discussion with the class on winning and losing. Throw out a few ideas yourself – a tug-of-war, exam results pinned to a noticeboard, the end of a race, a war, an election, the football pools. Discuss people's reactions to winning and losing – good and bad winners and losers. What about the reactions of the winners' and losers' families and friends? Don't discuss the subject to death, however – leave something to the imagination. Divide the class into groups of about six and ask them to prepare a piece on winning and losing.

Gangs

Each group is a gang with its own set of rules. In order to gain admittance to the gang the prospective member has to show initiative or carry out some feat acceptable to the rest.

The Imaginary Invention

Start by talking about different inventions – Thomas Edison's light bulb, the speak-your-weight machine, an imaginary electronic gadget. Divide the class into groups of about six and set them the brief of devising their very own imaginary invention. Each member of the group will be an integral part of the invention – apart from the spokesperson who will explain its use and demonstrate its workings to the rest of the class. All inventions must, of course, be named and explanations and demonstrations carried out thoroughly realistically.

Accident

A crowd gathers to watch the aftermath of an accident (the crowd can be anything from a group of six to the whole class). The teacher specifies the kind of accident that has taken place – it could be a road accident, a fall, a fire. The crowd reacts as the teacher relates what is happening. The teacher can further direct the group by freezing and spotlighting when necessary. Make sure that the crowd drifts in (and out) gradually and don't let them get too 'busy'.

A useful follow-up would be to discuss what you would really do in such circumstances. Perhaps you can bring in some first-aid tips as well as detailing the emergency procedure of dialling 999 for fire, police or ambulance.

2

Channelling Creativity

Everyone has talent in some field. It is a myth that it is only possessed by a small minority of gifted people. Every young individual has the potential to do many different things, given the opportunities and education. Equally, early ability can be stifled by lack of opportunity and encouragement. It's like the parable of the talents – you need to work at your talent rather than bury it in the ground.

Talent is developed by broadening people's minds and by training to improve their skills, while at the same time providing a secure emotional base so they are not afraid of failure. The key to it is praise, encouragement and improvement by gradual degrees, so that people are always being stretched but not stretched so far that they are likely to fail. Even when a high level of achievement has been reached, you have to keep in training in the arts, just as you do in sport, or else your ability will dissipate through lack of exercise. As Thomas Edison said, 'Genius is one per cent inspiration and ninety-nine per cent perspiration'.

A whole mix of talents are required for drama. Improvisation draws upon creative ability, and creativity is something that can be enhanced through training just like any other talent. Everyone has an imagination. The way to develop it is to release people's own inhibitions on using it, while at the same time teaching the disciplines which enable it to be channelled effectively.

LEADERSHIP

One of the social benefits of drama is that it gives participants experience of leadership and responsibility. Again, there is a myth that leadership ability is found only in a small number of people and is to be developed – or discouraged – in them only. On the contrary, leadership skills are something that everyone can, and should, learn. Sooner or later everyone has to be a leader – at work, in recreation, as a parent, or in the once-in-a-lifetime emergency where quick thinking, self-reliance and thinking of other people can make the difference between life and death.

Good leadership means the ability to communicate goals clearly, to take responsibility and to care for others, and listen and respond to them. Dictatorships don't usually last very long. One of the problems for a teacher is that in any class the same few people tend to emerge as the natural leaders. Because they are the only ones with leadership experience no one else can take their place effectively. If you wish to give more people a chance, it's no good throwing them in at the deep end. You have to introduce people to responsibility gradually.

The Imaginary Journey

This is an imagination exercise which can be done either in question-and-answer form with an individual or with the whole group. Start with 'I want you to close your eyes. Now look down at your feet. I want you to notice the pair of shoes you are wearing. Remember exactly what they look like, any details or marks on them. Now what sort of surface are the shoes standing on; is it a floor, or path, or pavement, or grass, or what? Without opening your eyes, look around you. Now you are going to go for a walk, it's quite a long way. Notice all the different things you see as you pass them.'

Give a few moments for the walk to continue, then say: 'In a moment you will come to a particular building. When you get to it I want you to stop and look at the outside and remember as many details as you can about the building. There's a sign on the building. Read to yourself what it says. Now you're going to go to the door of the building and, one way or another, go inside.'

And so it goes on. Maybe you will ask them to see something unexpected, or someone who (in the story) they love or hate. Maybe the person will ask them a question. What answer will they give? What will happen next? Maybe they will see a book, open it at a given page, count down a certain number of lines and read what it says.

The possibilities are endless and you can go on indefinitely. Everyone's story will be different and, if recounted, some of them will be remarkable. The exercise shows that everyone has untapped powers of imagination; because you've started with something very ordinary – the shoes – the class are more likely to use their imagination unselfconsciously.

FOSTERING CREATIVITY

In any group doing improvisation work, some of the students will want to start devising their own plays, drawing on the resources of imagination that improvisation has revealed. It is at this point, when groups start forming to work on their own projects, often in their own time, that advice from a teacher can be particularly valuable. This will often come in the form of comments on work you are seeing. What you say to the group about one of their plays, whether in performance or rehearsal, should always be positive and encouraging, but never fail to say anything that needs to be said to improve the play. While being specific, always try to point the general application of any points you make so that people will take them on board for other occasions.

What are the ingredients of a good play? It must have a strong plot and believable characters, and it should say something, perhaps in an original way. A 'twist' is often very effective and humour is another good ingredient to include.

When dealing with the *writing* of a play (even if it's a devised play that has not actually been written down), start with the basic idea. Is it an original theme or a hackneyed one? Has it been handled in an unusual way? Are there any unexpected dramatic moments or is it all too predictable? Does the play have a good, satisfying shape, a beginning, a middle and an end, with strategically placed turning-points? Are the scenes developed enough and do we get to know the characters as much as we would like to? Or are some of the scenes 'milked' and in need of editing? Is there a good, strong ending? Does the play have something worthwhile to say? A play doesn't necessarily need to have a message, certainly not at the expense of having credible characters, but if it comments on a moral or social or political question, then that gives the audience something to think about.

Scenarios

This is an exercise in devising ideas for plays. Divide the class into groups of about six and appoint a spokesperson for each group. Allow a few minutes for each group to think of an idea, then one by one they will tell the rest of the class a scenario or 'treatment' for a play: the theme, the location, an outline of the plot, the main characters, any turning-points and how it would be staged — and of course they must give it a title. Comment on any good points in each one and allow a brief discussion so that members of the class can suggest any additions they may have. The object of the exercise is to give practice in developing and moulding ideas, and, as it's done fairly quickly and they are 'throw-away' ideas that don't matter, the class should be able to work in an uninhibited way.

This can also be done as a solo idea, or with the scenarios being written down, but not more than half a page on each. Sometimes a scenario can be chosen, developed and acted out. Sometimes they may turn into full-scale plays.

DIRECTION

At this stage directing often goes hand in hand with writing, and you will often find collaborations with two people sharing both roles. Particular points to comment on in direction are a choice of a particular style for a play, the casting (in a group that has worked together for a while there's a tendency for individuals to drop into stock character roles), and whether the acting area has been used to good visual effect. Pace — simply the rate at which events happen — is vitally important. It needs to be varied in a way appropriate to the action. Dramatic tension needs to be maintained. Characters in a play need thinking time, and so does the audience. In particular, the opening of any play sets an audience a riddle. What is being represented? Who are the people? Where? When? How does each relate to the others? The audience has got to work all this out. Too many characters introduced at once or a muddled opening and you will lose its attention.

No play can be developed without a great deal of teamwork, and different individuals will develop in different roles within the team. It's not usually a good idea for writers or directors to appear in their own plays. The work load is too heavy and it is very difficult to see things from the points of view of both director and performer at the same time.

Comment on the work of the non-acting members of the team. If you have stage lighting it needs to be used to illuminate the actors effectively and, perhaps, to isolate one part of the acting area from its surroundings. Brightness, direction and colour effects need to be chosen to represent the place (indoors, outdoors) and time of day or night, and also, possibly, to represent the emotional atmosphere of the play. Lighting changes and effects usually need to be unobtrusive so that they do their work without the audience being too aware of them, and often the most economical use of stage lighting is the most effective. A simple piece of stage-lighting 'grammar' is that a fade tends to leave the audience expecting another scene to follow, while a black-out will normally cue their applause.

If it is a play with music, whether live or from records, similar principles apply. The music needs to be skilfully chosen for its associations and emotional effects without giving the game away about the plot. It is important to use enough of any incidental music; it takes time for an audience to tune into it and have its mood affected – just the odd line or two of a pop song is not sufficient. Records need to be cued accurately at the right moment so that the audience does not hear any unwanted 'funny noises'. If music is being used under speech in a play the level needs to be low enough for the words still to be heard. When music is faded out, it needs to be done musically, ending at the end of a musical phrase or a line of a song.

Other matters that need to be attended to are costume, props and the set. It is easy to think of productions where spectacular use of any of these has made an enormous contribution to the whole, but it is important to remember that they are there to serve the play and not to distract from it. So, unless something striking can be produced that will add to the overall impact of the play, it is better to aim for costume, props and set that are sufficient to create the effect required in the minds of the audience, rather than try to emulate lavishly budgeted West End productions.

PROFESSIONALISM

In all your comments on the group's work, show that you are looking for professionalism in everything they do, not because you are necessarily producing professional actors, but in order to encourage them to be *professional people*: people who do things the right way and as well as possible, are reliable and get on with those they are working with. A good concentration exercise is to have the members of a class all close their eyes and concentrate and prepare themselves by thinking of all the words beginning with the letter 'p' that go towards being professional people: punctuality, preparation, persistence, poise, practice, perfection, patience – we are sure there are many more!

CRITICISM

Criticism can be enormously helpful as a general teaching tool as well as to improve a particular piece of work, but it must always be constructive, never destructive. The teacher's praise rather than punishment produces better results on the whole, and when negative comments have to be made they should be framed as kindly as possible. Young people are usually very fair and often generous when commenting on the work of their peers. Encourage this and clamp down on anything destructive. It is up to you to create the right atmosphere, so that people can give of themselves in their work without the fear of being slapped in the face for their pains. Destructive criticism can be a great spectator sport, but, like all blood sports, it is better not to be the victim. Nevertheless, learning to take criticism, particularly if it is well justified, is an important lesson as well.

SHARING

One of the keys to groups working together cohesively is sharing. Learning to share is vitally important. Sharing and competitiveness are not at opposite poles. The essence of good sportsmanship is that people can compete with one another and be all the better friends for it. One of the essential steps in learning to share with people is getting to know them, and learning how to get to know them − sharing their experiences, enjoyment, ideas, problems, recommendations, and so forth. A good way of developing this in a group is, after starting the class with a physical and verbal warm-up, to do some quick 'sharing ideas', getting people to swap partners and so forth so that they will not be working with the people they are most familiar with.

Sharing Ideas

Here are some sharing ideas that can be used with the whole class working together, usually in pairs, and then some being individually 'spotlit'.

Recipes

'In twos share a recipe − it can be a main course or a pudding. I'll allow two minutes of "talking heads" than I'll either hear one person's own recipe or, more difficult, the new recipe he or she has just heard!'

Fact Finding

'In twos − two minutes only to find out as many facts about each other as you can. You *must* find out at least six facts each. It might be the colour of your toothbrush, your mum's first name, the number on your front door. Find out as many facts about each other in two minutes as you can. Then we'll test some of you. Starting from *now*!'

The Best and Worst Thing . . .

'In twos, find out the best thing that ever happened to you and the worst thing that ever happened to you. I'll give you one minute to tell each other, then we'll all hear about it.'

Sundays

'In twos or threes, tell each other what you do on a Sunday from when you get up in the morning to when you go to bed at night. You are forbidden to use the word "boring".'

Hobbies

'In twos or threes, tell each other three hobbies you enjoy doing, *not* including watching television. Not that I've got anything against television as such − but there are other things and TV is so instant you don't have to *do* anything, just sit down and switch on. So − three hobbies, please, not including television.'

Pocket Money

'In twos or threes, tell each other how much pocket money you get and what you do with it. I'll be interested to hear if anyone puts theirs into savings.'

Rooms

'In twos, describe to each other either your bedroom or any other room in your house. Let's have some vivid descriptions, please. I'd like to be able to "see" the room in my mind's eye.'

Three Jobs

'In threes, I'd like you each to describe three jobs you'd seriously contemplate doing when you leave school, and the reasons why you'd like to do them.'

News

'In twos, I want you to exchange three pieces of news − a piece of family news, a piece of local news and a piece of worldwide news. Let's hear about something that has really captured your attention.'

Mum, Dad, Nan, Old Uncle Tom Cobbleigh . . .

'In twos, I want you to describe in detail a member of your family, either your mum, dad, nan, brother, sister or anyone else. I'd like to hear about what they look like, their personality and character, any idiosyncrasies or peculiarities they might have, their hobbies, how you get on with them, and so on.'

Your Friend

'In twos, describe a friend of yours. Tell your partner all about him or her — looks, personality, hobbies, what you do together ... I'll give you two minutes and then we'll hear about some of them individually. Start with their name. It's not a guessing game.'

Recommendations

'I want to go round the room hearing your recommendations. You can recommend a book, a film, a television or radio programme, or a theatre production. I want each of you to suggest something that you got a lot of enjoyment out of and tell us why you liked it so much. If it's a book, give the title, author and a sentence or two to say what it's about.'

From arts recommendations, you could try other subjects such as shops, restaurants, places to go. . . .

Resolutions

'I want to go round the room and hear each person give from one to three New Year resolutions. Now, some people feel that if you break a resolution once you might as well give up trying to keep it altogether; I'd call that defeatism. As the song says, you should "Pick yourself up, dust yourself down and start all over again". Let's hear them.' This can be developed by suggesting a New Year resolution for someone else.

Holiday Reading

'In twos, recommend two pieces of holiday reading to each other. Give the title, author and a line or two on the subject matter.'

Back to School

'In twos, tell each other about three specific things you did in the school holidays.'

Lost and Found

'In twos, tell each other of any experiences you've had when you lost something important (perhaps a contact lens or a gold ring) and if you ever found anything valuable – in which case, I wonder what you did with it. Did you take it to the police station or was it "finders keepers, losers weepers"? If you haven't lost or found anything, I'm sure you know someone who has.'

Presents

'In twos, swap ideas about presents. First, tell each other about a present you would like to receive; next, a present you'd like to give; and then three presents under £5 suitable for your mum or dad.'

A Pleasant Surprise, an Unpleasant Shock

'In twos, tell each other of a pleasant surprise you've had and of an unpleasant shock. If you can think of neither of these that you have experienced personally, you may tell us of ones that have happened to people you know.'

Discoveries

'In twos, tell each other of two discoveries, big or small, that you have made in the last year. It could be a household hint, a little-known fact, or an unusual place to visit – in other words, any piece of interesting knowledge or know-how. Then I'd like you to share them with all of us.'

The Real and the Imaginary Problem

'In twos, tell each other a real problem and an imaginary problem; your partner has to guess which is the real problem and which is the imaginary one. Later on the whole class will try and decipher which is true and which is false.'

Dreams

'In twos, tell each other about two dreams – one that you've really had and one you've made up. Can your partner guess which is which?'

Group Work

Sharing Ideas can be done with larger groups of people as well.

Favourite Things

Form groups of from six to eight who one at a time will tell one another a few of their favourite things – books, places, shops, dinners, pets, hobbies, sport, puddings, magazines, records, jokes, films, etc.

The Inner and the Outer Circle

This is a good ice-breaking exercise. Divide the class into pairs, and tell the pairs to form a circle facing each other, making an inner and an outer circle. The partners get to know one another or, if they already do so, catch up on each other's news. After a short while, the teacher either rings a bell, blows a whistle, or calls out 'All change'. Then the inner circle stays put, the outer circle moves one step to the right and the new partners start all over again, and so on.

This is an ideal exercise to warm up a new group or to welcome people back after the holidays.

Another way of working in groups is to split a class into sections who will prepare work on a given theme to show one another later in the session. Groups can be self-selecting but it is often a good idea to split people in an arbitrary way so that they get used to working with different people. Appoint group leaders who have a chairman's casting vote to resolve any differences. The art in this kind of group work lies in finding an initial brief that will inspire good drama.

Subjects

A subject of general interest may be chosen for discussion; improvisation can follow on from this. It is often a good idea to suggest a title – one that provides a stimulus but not a limitation. For example, a discussion on 'The Family (Conventional and Unconventional)' might be followed by improvisations with the title 'One Family'; a discussion on 'Mental Illness' might be followed by work on 'The Case of XYZ (a person's name)'; one on 'What Makes a Good Holiday' might be commented on by 'Two Weeks in ABC (the name of a resort)'. If the title is made optional, you have the best of both worlds: you have provided a suggestion but if the group has a better idea your suggestion can be overruled.

A similar format is to discuss a present-day issue and then use improvisations to project it into what may possibly, or even improbably, happen in the future, under the general title 'The Surprising Future of . . .'. Thus a discussion on entertainment, or a subject connected with it, could be followed by improvisations on 'The Surprising Future of Entertainment', and similarly with love, war, childhood, and so on.

Locations

Alternatively, you can simply give them a location. One that works particularly well is 'Kitchen Scenes'. Another is 'Office Scenes'. Another that works well for pairs rather than groups is 'Bedroom Scenes' — bedtime conversations between husband and wife, parent and child, or any others who share a bedroom.

Titles

Another way is to give a brief and a title with no obvious connection between the two. The brief might be that a chosen subject should be brought into the play in some way or other — old age, science, smoking, foreign languages. The title can be one of a series you have made up and written down on slips of paper, or a title hybridized from a couple of well-known television programmes. A fun variation on this is to choose, say, the titles of a current hit record, a top-rated TV programme, a big box-office film and a best-selling novel. Give one to each of the groups. They can do any improvisation they like that fits this title, but it must bear *no* resemblance to the original work that bears the same title.

Festivals

As group work develops it is often a good idea to have a target for everyone to work towards. We have found an end-of-term festival very successful — see the section on Festivals in Chapter 4.

TOTAL THEATRE

This is another form of group work in which the entire class works together (if there are too many, divide it in half). Give them the brief of what the overall situation is, then each of them chooses a character who could be in that situation and, without further preparation, improvisation begins, interrupted only if you want to freeze the action and spotlight a particular set of characters for a while, in the same way as in 'Table Talk' (Chapter 1).

Examples of settings that could be used are:

    A Youth Club on an Ordinary Evening   Start with a show of hands to make sure you have the right proportion of youth workers to members. The action begins when the person with the keys opens up the doors and ends when the same person locks them again.

    A School Playground at Break Time   From bell to bell. You can put in a few extra details such as a staff-room that overlooks the playground, or a wall that backs on to somebody's back garden.

The Staff Christmas Party of a Large Business   It is held at a big hotel and everybody is there, from the cleaners to the managing director, and from different areas – factories, offices, sales reps, and so on. The seating plan mixes people together so they can get to know one another, and there's plenty of drink flowing. Everyone is going to let their hair down. This scenario might be helped by having the characters introduce themselves, name and position, one by one. It could be tailed by asking for scenes involving selected characters in the hotel corridors afterwards.

A Marriage Guidance Group   The group is split into couples, who decide on an outline of their age, background, family, and the problems they may have. The group is led by a counsellor and we are going to see the characters arrive and discuss their own and other people's problems. Perhaps this one can finish with the couples being seen in turn on their way home together.

The Friends Circle   This is a bit like Alcoholics Anonymous or Weightwatchers. Each member has a personal problem or idiosyncrasy that makes his or her life difficult. They meet once a week and talk about how they've coped in the previous week. You might appoint a leader, or not. Alternatively, to make it more of an exercise, you might have them draw cards with the problems written on them: alcoholic, insomniac, overweight, paranoid.

For these improvisations to be successful, subtlety in characterization and generous, unassertive acting are essential. All the situations have potential for humour and they must be played straight and not sent up. This is particularly true when comedy is the intention. Often you can finish off the piece of work by interviewing some of the characters, in character, asking them to give their account of what happened, how they feel about some of the other people, and so on.

3

Umbrella Themes

To take an umbrella theme for the term is to choose a subject, be it
literary or cultural, from which you can draw material for use
throughout the term. For example, if your umbrella theme is Aesop's
Fables you take a different fable each week which will provide a
substantial part of the material for that session. After you have
introduced the fable of the week you can explain the context and
background and have a short discussion with the class on any points
it raises. The fable can then be used as a starting-off point for
improvisation, situation drama and plays.

As well as supplying good dramatic material, the subjects chosen
are areas in which students can benefit from increasing their general
knowledge. The umbrella theme provides an orderly way of working
on them. This concise way of dealing with subjects gives a target, a
shape and an identity to your term's work.

It is very useful to display your umbrella theme of the term on
your notice board. For example:

FABLE OF THE WEEK

The Boy Who Called Wolf

SPOTLIGHT ON

Credibility

PROVERBS

Proverbs are old and wise sayings which make excellent material for
discussion and improvisation. Take 'A friend in need is a friend
indeed'. Start with a discussion on friendship. Talk about the qualities
that make a good friendship – loyalty, confidentiality, humour,
compatibility, or indeed the attraction of opposites. What is most
important in a friendship? What makes friendship last? What is the

best thing a friend ever did for you? What is the best thing you ever did for a friend? What is the worst?

Continue on these lines until you're ready to set up an improvisation on the week's proverb, possibly using an optional first line – 'Some friend you turned out to be', or 'I really appreciated what you did for me yesterday'. You can do an assortment of duologues on this theme, with or without a first line as starting-point. This can be developed further into a piece of situation drama or a related improvisation.

Here is a list of proverbs that work well:

> Practice makes perfect
> Never judge a book by its cover
> Don't bite the hand that feeds you
> The early bird catches the worm
> There are no roses without dung
> A leopard never changes its spots
> Self-praise is no praise
> Lend money, lose a friend
> Necessity is the mother of invention
> When the cat's away the mice will play
> Honesty is the best policy
> There's no accounting for taste
> One man's meat is another man's poison
> What the eye doesn't see the heart doesn't grieve over
> Actions speak louder than words
> Don't spoil the ship for a ha'p'orth o' tar
> Money is the root of all evil
> Forbidden fruit tastes twice as sweet
> Criticism is the only tool that works all the better for being blunt
> Once a man gets above himself he rarely rises any higher

MOTTOES

A motto, to quote the dictionary, is a 'saying adapted as rule of conduct: short inscribed sentence: word or sentence on heraldic crest'. Here are some ready-made for improvisation:

> 'Be prepared' (Guides, Scouts)
> 'Lend a hand' (Brownies)
> 'Who dares wins' (SAS)

'Rise and shine'
'Lente sed attente' – 'Slowly but carefully'
'Ambition sans envie' – 'Ambition without envy'
'Let them talk'
'Fortune favours the brave'
'A bonis ad meliora' – 'From good things to better'
'My word is my bond' (Stock Exchange)
'Nil desperandum' – 'Never despair'
'Manners Makyth Man' (William of Wykeham, 1324–1404)
'Nulla rosa sine spinis' – 'No rose without thorns'
'Audio sed taceo' – 'I hear but say nothing'
'Constantia in ardua' – 'Perseverance against difficulty'
'Respect faith, but doubt is what gives you an education'
'Love makes the world go round'
'Never put off till tomorrow what can be done today'
'Do as you would be done by'
'Reality before theatricality' (East 15 Acting School)

POEM OF THE WEEK

Compile a list of favourite poems – your own and the class's. From the list, choose poems that have aspects that can be highlighted through improvisation. For example, in 'Jim' by Hilaire Belloc you could home in on *caution*, while in 'The Snare' by the Irish poet James Stephens you could choose the subject of cruelty to animals.

Remember to put on your notice-board under 'POEM OF THE WEEK' its title and the poet's name and dates. Of course, different age-groups will appreciate different poems and, indeed, different teachers will find different aspects to highlight in each poem. Some poems won't work because they are too abstract, but here is a list of ones that have worked well for us.

'Matilda', Hilaire Belloc (1870–1953)
'Lies', Yevgeni Yevtushenko (born 1933)
'If', Rudyard Kipling (1865–1936)
'When You Are Old', W. B. Yeats (1865–1939)
'For Anne Gregory', W. B. Yeats (1865–1939)
'Little Billee', William Makepeace Thackeray (1811–63)
'Lucy Gray', William Wordsworth (1770–1850)
'Lord Ullin's Daughter', Thomas Campbell (1777–1850)
'Death the Leveller', James Shirley (1596–1666)
'Not Waving But Drowning', Stevie Smith (1905–71)

'A Crabbit Old Woman', Anon.
'My Mother Said', Anon.
'The Donkey', G. K. Chesterton (1874–1936)
'Gus, The Theatre Cat', T. S. Eliot (1888–1965)

QUOTATION OF THE WEEK

The pithy quote is a very good source for interpretation through discussion and improvisation, in the same way as proverbs, mottoes and poems. Here is a list.

'Love thy neighbour as thyself' (Leviticus; St Matthew)
'A soft answer turneth away wrath; but grievous words stir up anger' (Book of Proverbs)
'Physician, heal thyself' (St Luke)
'Sed quis custodiet ipsos custodes' – 'But who will guard the guards themselves?' (Juvenal)
'Strange how potent cheap music is' (Noel Coward, 1899–1973)
'To be successful at anything you have to have the guts to be hated' (Bette Davis, twentieth-century film actress)
'Genius is one per cent inspiration, and ninety-nine per cent perspiration' (Thomas Edison, 1849–1931)
'A man, Sir, should keep his friendship in constant repair' (Dr Samuel Johnson, 1709–84)
'The struggle in my trapeze act is the same struggle that I feel in my life – the struggle for balance' (Wendy Parkman, The Pickles Family Circus, 1980s)
'To err is human, to forgive, divine' (Alexander Pope, 1688–1744)
'A little learning is a dangerous thing' (Alexander Pope, 1688–1744)
'Two things I can't stand – one is if actors are late, the second is if they cannot learn their lines' (Otto Preminger, twentieth-century film director)
'Liberty means responsibility and that's why most men dread it' (George Bernard Shaw, 1856–1950)
'One must love Art and not oneself in Art' (Konstantin Stanislavsky, 1865–1938)
'All acting is giving and receiving' (Konstantin Stanislavsky, 1865–1938)
'The buck stops here' (Harry S Truman, 1884–1972)

'If you can't stand the heat – stay out of the kitchen' (Harry S
  Truman, 1884–1972)
'There will always be people that don't go for your chemistry
  – make sure they go for your skill' (Orson Welles,
  1915–85, to Joan Plowright)
'There is only one thing worse than being talked about, and
  that is not being talked about' (Oscar Wilde, 1854–1900)

SHAKESPEAREAN QUOTATION OF THE WEEK

Shakespeare is another good source of quotations for improvisation.
We have chosen a list of popular ones, many of which are now part
of the language, such as 'What's in a name?' You may need to explain
some of the Elizabethan English. Also, you will need to describe
where the quotation comes from in the text – this will be helpful in
introducing the plays.

'My salad days,
When I was green in judgment' (*Antony and Cleopatra*)
'Though it be honest, it is never good
To bring bad news' (*Antony and Cleopatra*)
'Frailty, thy name is woman!' (*Hamlet*)
'The lady doth protest too much, methinks' (*Hamlet*)
'All that live must die
Passing through nature to eternity' (*Hamlet*)
'Neither a borrower nor a lender be,
For loan oft loses both itself and friend' (*Hamlet*)
'The better part of valour is discretion' (*Henry IV, Part 1*)
'If all the year were playing holidays
To sport would be as tedious as to work
But when they seldom come they wished for come' (*Henry IV,
  Part 1*)
'Self-love, my liege, is not so vile a sin as Self-neglecting'
  (*Henry V*)
'The fault, dear Brutus, is not in our stars
But in ourselves, that we are underlings' (*Julius Caesar*)
'That was the most unkindest cut of all' (*Julius Caesar*)
'Ambition should be made of sterner stuff' (*Julius Caesar*)
'It is a wise father that knows his own child' (*Merchant of
  Venice*)
'The course of true love never did run smooth' (*A Midsummer
  Night's Dream*)

'Your play needs no excuse' (*A Midsummer Night's Dream*)
'O! beware, my lord, of jealousy,
It is the green-eyed monster which doth mock
The meat it feeds on' (*Othello*)
'What's in a name? That which we call a rose
By any other name would smell as sweet' (*Romeo and Juliet*)
'Parting is such sweet sorrow
That I shall say good-night till it be morrow' (*Romeo and Juliet*)
'Condemn the fault and not the actor of it?' (*Measure for Measure*)
'Nothing will come of nothing' (*King Lear*)
'All's well that ends well' (*All's Well that Ends Well*)

SHAKESPEAREAN PLAY OF THE WEEK

The unfamiliar Elizabethan language is often the stumbling-block when it comes to understanding Shakespeare. Start by telling the story of the plot in your own words, allowing the characters to come through as real flesh-and-blood people. Discussion, improvisation and text work follow in that order. Then, when the class see a performance of the play, knowing the plot and dramatic content, they are more likely to appreciate the language in which it is written.

But first some background notes.

William Shakespeare (1564–1616) was born in Stratford-upon-Avon on 23 April, which is also St George's Day. He attended the local grammar school – the King's New School of Stratford-upon-Avon – but did not go to university. At eighteen he married Anne Hathaway, who was eight years his senior, and they had three children, Susanna, and twins, Hamnet and Judith. Hamnet died at eleven. When he was in his twenties Shakespeare moved to London and joined James Burbage's company of actors, the Lord Chamberlain's Men. As actors in the sixteenth century were otherwise classified as 'rogues and vagabonds', patronage from nobility was necessary.

William Shakespeare started as an actor with James Burbage's son Richard but soon wrote plays for the company. In all he wrote thirty-eight plays – comedies, tragedies, and historical plays. He wrote some poems, most notably *Venus and Adonis* and *The Rape of Lucrece*. And he wrote one hundred and fifty-four sonnets (fourteen-line poems), the most popular being 'Shall I Compare Thee to a Summer's Day?' Shakespeare retired to Stratford-upon-Avon in 1611, a prosperous man, and died there on his fifty-second birthday.

Famous contemporaries of Shakespeare, apart from Queen Elizabeth I and James and Richard Burbage, were the playwright Christopher Marlowe, born in the same year, 1564, but tragically killed in a drunken brawl in Deptford, London, in 1593; the actor Edward Alleyn; the clowns Will Kempe, Richard Tarleton and Robert Armin; and the playwrights Ben Jonson, Richard Greene, Thomas Kyd and Beaumont and Fletcher.

The Elizabethan theatre was open to the sky with a raised apron stage which had a trapdoor in the middle. Behind the apron stage was a wall with curtained doorways giving access to an inner stage and the dressing-rooms. The wall supported a gallery for musicians or the actors themselves and a tower above housed machinery. The area above the stage was called 'the heavens' and the area below, 'the hell'. There was no scenery but rich costumes and plenty of stage properties. There were no women on the Elizabethan stage; their parts were played by males. As a member of the audience, where you sat (or stood) depended on your pocket. The 'groundlings' stood round the apron stage for one penny – the best part of a pound in today's money. People with more money would sit on seats looking down on the stage from one of the galleries. The richest people had private boxes, or stools round the edge of the stage itself. A trumpet call announced that the play was about to begin and a flag was flown during performances, which usually took place early in the afternoon. The theatres were built outside the city walls, and most of Shakespeare's plays were performed in the Globe, which Shakespeare refers to as the 'wooden O'.

Here are five of Shakespeare's Plays with storylines briefly summarized and 'spotlight' points detailed.

1   Hamlet, Prince of Denmark

Spotlight on 'Revenge'

The ghost of his father appears to Hamlet and tells him that he was poisoned by Hamlet's uncle, Claudius, who has since married Hamlet's mother, Queen Gertrude. The play tells how Hamlet seeks revenge for this. He appears to go mad and this, in turn, drives his lady Ophelia insane. Hamlet asks a company of players to perform a play with a plot similar to his father's murder and Claudius reacts in a way that proves his guilt. Ophelia drowns herself and her brother Laertes swears revenge. He fights a duel with Hamlet and both of them die, as do Gertrude and Claudius.

Mention other features of the play such as Hamlet's soliloquy 'To be or not to be ...', or Polonius's words of wisdom 'Neither a borrower nor a lender be,/For loan oft loses both itself and friend.'

Discuss the spotlight subject 'revenge'. Do you believe in an eye for an eye or turning the other cheek? In soliloquy, monologue or duologue, set up improvisations with the first line

'I'm going to get my own back on her/him.'

Choose a piece of text to work from, for example, the Ophelia–Polonius duologue (Act II scene i), where Ophelia has been frightened by Hamlet's madness and seeks her father's help.

2   Romeo and Juliet

Spotlight on 'Forbidden Fruit'

The Montagues and the Capulets are rival families in Verona. Romeo, Montague's heir, falls in love with Juliet, Capulet's daughter, at a masked ball. They meet by night and Friar Lawrence marries them secretly the following afternoon. Tybalt, Juliet's cousin, challenges Romeo to a fight. Romeo refuses but his friend Mercutio, enraged, accepts the challenge and is fatally wounded. Romeo kills Tybalt in revenge. He is banished and Juliet is ordered to marry Paris, a nobleman. Friar Lawrence devises a plan by which Juliet, by taking a potion, can feign death, thus avoiding marriage to Paris. He sends word to Romeo to come and rescue Juliet from Capulet's tomb but before this can happen Romeo has received a message that Juliet is dead. Romeo hurries to the tomb, kills Paris and takes poison. Juliet awakens and, finding Romeo dead, kills herself. The Montagues and the Capulets are reconciled over the bodies of Romeo and Juliet.

No discussion of *Romeo and Juliet* would be complete without reference to the famous balcony scene between the 'star-crossed lovers'.

Discuss the spotlight subject 'forbidden fruit'. Do you think that Romeo and Juliet would have been so passionately attracted to one another had their parents approved of their relationship? Does forbidden fruit taste twice as sweet? If so, why? In twos, as parent and offspring, use the first and second lines:

'I forbid you to go out with that boy/girl'
'But why?'

An apt piece of text work would be the duologue between Juliet and the Nurse (Act II scene v), in which we see the Nurse teasing Juliet, holding back to the end the good news that Friar Lawrence will marry her to Romeo.

3   Julius Caesar

Spotlight on 'Conspiracy'

The conspirators, Cassius, Casca and Brutus, plot to murder Julius Caesar because they believe he is growing too powerful. A soothsayer warns Caesar to beware the Ides of March (15 March), but he goes to the Capitol where he is stabbed to death. His body is carried to the Forum, where Brutus justifies the assassination to the mob; then Mark Antony addresses them and turns them against the conspirators. Civil war breaks out between the triumvirate (Mark Antony, Octavius and Lepidus) and the conspirators. They will meet in battle at Philippi; Caesar's ghost appears to Brutus telling him that he will see him again at Philippi. The battle lost, Cassius orders a servant to stab him, and Brutus runs on his own sword. Mark Antony delivers his epitaph.

A scene that provides excellent discussion material is the one in which Cinna the poet is murdered by the mob just because he has the same name as Cinna the conspirator – an example of mob mentality, when a crowd will behave collectively in a way they would not do as individuals. Another discussion subject that comes up is that of ambition. Who was the more ambitious, Caesar or the conspirators? How far should one pursue ambition at the expense of others?

Discuss the spotlight subject 'conspiracy' – plotting, paranoia, bad-mouthing, slandering. In twos, use the first line:

'You've been plotting against, me, haven't you?'

A good piece of text work is Mark Antony's famous speech in the forum: 'Friends, Romans, countrymen . . .' (Act III scene ii). Brutus has made the mistake of allowing Mark Antony to speak after him. Without overtly speaking against the conspirators, Mark Antony skilfully manipulates the mob's feelings and turns it against them.

4   Othello

Spotlight on: 'The Green-Eyed Monster'

The three protagonists of the piece are Othello, the black Moor of Venice, his wife Desdemona and Iago, one of his officers. Iago is consumed by envy of Othello. Othello is sent to govern Cyprus, where his new lieutenant, Cassio, egged on by Iago, gets drunk and is disgraced. Iago, who has hinted to Othello that Desdemona is unfaithful to him, suggests to Cassio that he should ask Desdemona to intercede for him. Iago persuades his wife Emilia to steal Desdemona's handkerchief, which he plants on Cassio. Iago then points out to Othello that Cassio has given it to his mistress, Bianca. He inflames Othello to the point where Othello swears he will kill Desdemona. He smothers her in bed. Emilia comes in and, horrified by Desdemona's death, reveals what Iago has done. Iago stabs her. Othello kills himself and Iago is taken away to be tortured.

As with Shylock in *The Merchant of Venice*, some of the racial references to Othello are abusive. Nevertheless, Othello is a majestic character who transcends stereotypes. The subject of how black people are depicted in the media down to the present day is a very fertile one for discussion.

Discuss the subject 'the green-eyed monster' – jealousy:

> 'O! beware, my lord of jealousy,
> It is the green-eyed monster which doth mock
> The meat it feeds on.'

Take it from different points of view in turn as a monologue *en masse*. First from Othello's point of view:

> 'I have proof you were with Cassio.'

Next take it from Desdemona's point of view:

> 'Othello, you've got it all wrong!'

From Iago's point of view:

> 'Othello, not being horrible or anything ...'

Now from your own point of view:

> 'Othello, you are blinded by jealousy ...'

Simple modern day duologues can be set up using various first lines to depict the subject of jealousy, for example:

> 'Look here, everyone knows you're just madly jealous of
> Tony ...'

For text work there is a very powerful duologue between Iago and Othello at the beginning of Act IV scene i, in which Iago, making great play with the handkerchief, is taunting and cruel to Othello's wretchedness and despair.

5   A Midsummer Night's Dream

Spotlight on 'Love at First Sight'

The play is set in an imaginary Athens. It has three parallel stories: the romantic story of two pairs of aristocratic lovers, the exploits of the immortals (the fairy folk), and the comical antics of the mechanicals (a group of tradesmen rehearsing a play). Hermia has been ordered to marry Demetrius but she refuses as she is in love with Lysander. They decide to elope together, meeting in a wood. Meanwhile, her friend Helena, who is in love with Demetrius, has told him about their plan, and he too goes to the wood, followed by Helena. The wood is the haunt of fairy folk and Oberon and Titania, king and queen of the fairies, have quarrelled over a changeling boy. Oberon orders Puck (also known as Robin Goodfellow) to fetch a flower, the juice of which, squeezed on the eyelids of Titania, will make her fall in love with whoever she first sees on awakening. He also orders him to squeeze it on Demetrius's eyes, but by mistake Puck anoints Lysander, who when he awakens falls in love with Helena. The mechanicals meet in the wood to rehearse their play and by magical means Puck puts an ass's head on Bottom the weaver. Titania wakes up and promptly falls in love with him. Finally, Oberon and Puck remove all the spells and Bottom awakes, as if from the strangest dream. The play 'Pyramus and Thisbe' is performed at the palace – farcically. Midnight strikes and all retire to bed, leaving the world to the fairies.

Point out that 'A Midsummer Night's Dream' is full of *dramatic irony*, which is when the audience know something that a character in the play is unaware of. A subject that can follow on from the play is 'dreams'. Both their content and meaning provide good material for discussion and improvisation.

The spotlight subject, 'love at first sight', makes a good talking-point. What first attracts you to someone? Looks? Personality? What makes for a good relationship? What makes a good partner for life? How do you feel about arranged marriages? Divide the class into pairs – they are best friends or girl-friend and boy-friend. Now, as Lysander says in the play, 'The course of true love never did run smooth' – the situation is that the friends or lovers have just had their very first quarrel. The first line is 'Well, what can I say?'

A suitable piece which demonstrates unrequited love is the

duologue between Demetrius and Helena in Act II scene i, starting with Demetrius's 'I love thee not, therefore pursue me not', and ending with Helena's 'I'll follow thee, and make a heaven of hell, To die upon the hand I love so well.'

THEATRE THROUGH THE AGES

This umbrella theme can be helped enormously if you make your own theatre time chart in advance. If you do so, it is well worth adding the main figures in literature, music, art, history, science and invention. Try not to see theatre in isolation, as it were, but in conjunction with the other arts, social history and, indeed, sciences. If that proves too academic then at least keep the literature section – theatre and literature walk hand in hand. Obviously you cannot go into the other subjects in any great depth; the idea is to form a bridge to other school subjects, so that they are not being studied in isolation.

Reference books, particularly on the history of British theatre, will need to be looked into before you embark on this project – an essential piece of homework.

Theatre through the ages can be conveniently divided into seven stages, though you might start with an introduction and end with a recapitulation.

On your notice-board, under the heading THEATRE THROUGH THE AGES, write: *This Week* (to be followed by the title of the week's stage), *Play of the Week* and then *Other Features*.

Stage 1

Stage 1 is 'Before 1000'. You might recommend the play *The Trojan Women* by Euripides and talk about the Greek and Roman theatre. *Other Features* might include Aesop's Fables and you might also mention Homer, Virgil and the long narrative poem Beowulf. Historically, Julius Caesar came to Britain in 55 BC, the Roman invasion of Britain took place in AD 43, and the Revolt of Boadicea was in AD 60. The emergence of Christianity was of immense significance. For your improvisation work you might take the subject of 'suffering' from *The Trojan Women* or read selected extracts from the play. There is a mass of material to be improvised or mimed from Aesop's Fables, so we have treated this as a separate theme.

Stage 2

Stage 2 is from the eleventh to the fifteenth century – medieval theatre. Liturgical or church drama in the shape of mystery plays (stories from the Bible), miracle plays (stories about the saints) and morality plays (about good versus evil) provides excellent material for improvisation and discussion. Recommend the play *Everyman*, anonymously written, about the struggle between Good and Evil and in which it is your good deeds that count in the end. *Other Features* might include Geoffrey Chaucer (*c.* 1340–1400) and *The Canterbury Tales*. Or you might like to home in on the Arthurian legends, Excalibur, the magic sword, the wizard Merlin, Lancelot and Queen Guinevere.

The great artists of the Renaissance such as Leonardo da Vinci (1452–1519) came at the end of this time and, historically, the Norman Conquest (1066), the Domesday Book (1086) and Magna Carta (1215) are of significance. Another dramatic figure of this period was Joan of Arc (1412–31), which might lead to some work on courage. (In fact, 'Heroes and Heroines' is another umbrella theme in its own right.) A good first line for an improvisation, using *Everyman* as your motivation, would be 'You know the difference between right and wrong.'

Stage 3

Stage 3 is the sixteenth century – Elizabethan theatre. William Shakespeare (1564–1616) is synonymous with the Elizabethan theatre and there are several of his plays you can recommend. *Romeo and Juliet* is particularly suitable for a teenage class. Christopher Marlowe was a direct contemporary of Shakespeare's, born in the same year, 1564, and tragically murdered in Deptford, south London in 1593. His three great plays, *Doctor Faustus*, *The Jew of Malta* and *Tamburlaine the Great*, all provide excellent dramatic material for readings or improvisations. The poet John Donne (1572–1631), who wrote the immortal line 'No man is an island', is also a good source for improvisation work.

Historically, there was the Reformation from 1517, Henry VIII, 1491–1547, and the Spanish Armada, 1588. Compare the Elizabethan theatre, which we have written about in the previous section, with the theatre today. In Elizabethan times theatres were disapproved of by the authorities, had to be built outside the city walls and were often closed because of the plague. Mention also the Italian *commedia dell'arte* - a marvellous combination of dancing, singing, mime, acrobatics, comedy and improvisation.

Stage 4

Stage 4 is the seventeenth century – Restoration theatre. You might recommend *The Way of the World* by William Congreve and talk about the 'comedy of manners' style, where wit and sometimes sarcasm is displayed while depicting people's manners and idiosyncrasies. Samuel Pepys is one of the century's most colourful figures. His diary, written in cipher, gives us vivid descriptions of the seventeenth-century theatre. He tells us that the seats of the theatre were not numbered or reserved but that servants could keep them for their masters. You might also talk about famous diaries, from Anne Frank's to Adrian Mole's. A good first line for duologue work might be 'How dare you read my diary', followed by soliloquies using the first line 'He/she's got a nerve . . .'. Historically the Gunpowder Plot, Guy Fawkes (1605), the Pilgrim Fathers (1620), Oliver Cromwell (1599–1658), the Plague (1665) and the Great Fire of London (1666) were some of the important events. The great scientists of the age were Galileo and Newton. Oliver Cromwell, the Lord Protector and a Puritan, was responsible for closing the theatres, and when Charles II came back to England the monarchy was restored. Thus this period is called Restoration theatre.

While in France, Charles II saw the early comedies of Molière and he was keen to see English theatres flourish again. The Theatre Royal, Drury Lane, was the most popular of the day. By now the theatres were roofed over so plays could be performed by artificial light, such as candles, torches and oil-lamps. Women appeared on the stage for the first time and Nell Gwyn, a former orange seller, was a well liked actress at Drury Lane. Inigo Jones introduced the proscenium, or picture-frame, stage. It had curtains and, because of the poor lighting, the stage was extended out into the audience – an apron stage.

Stage 5

And so, on to stage 5 – the eighteenth century. Recommend Richard Brinsley Sheridan's *The School for Scandal* or *The Rivals*. Sheridan, like William Congreve before him, and his contemporary, Oliver Goldsmith, wrote in the 'comedy of manners' style. Pantomime, a derivative of the Italian *commedia dell'arte*, with its spectacular elements, was popular. It was at this time that plays were put under the censorship of the Lord Chamberlain to ensure that nothing was being written against the government or the Crown. There is a lot of good improvisation and discussion work to be found in the subject of censorship. Take a duologue, parent and offspring, using the first line 'Don't you ever use that foul language in this house'.

Daniel Defoe and Jonathan Swift were great literary figures of the eighteenth century. This was known as the 'Age of Reason' and towards the end of the century came the beginning of the Industrial Revolution. Other points in the historical background include American Independence (1776), the French Revolution (1789) and Napoleon (1769–1821). This was the century of the great classical composers Bach (1685–1750), Handel (1685–1759) and Mozart (1756–91).

Stage 6

The nineteenth century is stage 6. Stage lighting made enormous improvements – first gaslight and then electric lighting, introduced at the Savoy Theatre in 1880. Machinery was used to make the stage sink or revolve. Scenery was lavish and the box set was popular. Music hall was a great success and Marie Lloyd ('A little of what you fancy does you good') a great favourite. Recommend *Pygmalion* by George Bernard Shaw, which has since become the musical *My Fair Lady*. The central characters – the cockney girl, Eliza Doolittle, and her mentor, Professor Henry Higgins, who teaches her to speak properly – should provide good material for improvisation and discussion.

Jane Austen was a great novelist of the nineteenth century. The life and works of Charles Dickens would be an excellent example for your *Other Features* category. The Romantic poets, Wordsworth, Coleridge, Byron, Keats and Shelley, will provide excellent material for poetry readings. Highly recommended is 'Lucy Grey' by Wordsworth, a poem about a little girl who gets lost in the snow, never to return. The century's leading composers include Beethoven and Brahms.

Historical events include the battles of Trafalgar (1805) and Waterloo (1815) and the Crimean War (1854–6). Many of the inventions which shape the modern world – the railways, the telephone, the car – first appeared in the nineteenth century and it was also an age of humanitarian and social advance; for example, slavery was abolished.

Stage 7

The seventh and last stage is the twentieth century – modern theatre.

47

You might recommend *Look Back in Anger* by John Osborne as your play of the week. The central character, Jimmy Porter, was the prototype of the 'angry young man'. He was angry about the class system in Britain. Ask the group what, if anything, makes them angry – a good first line for improvisation would be 'I'll tell you why I'm angry'. Give them a free rein to sound off on any subject. George Orwell, with his *Animal Farm* and *1984*, might be a candidate for the *Other Features* category. If you can lay your hands on any reproduction picture cards of Picasso's work they could be included in the project. The First World War (1914–18), the Russian Revolution (1917), the Second World War (1939–45) and Indian Independence (1947) are some of the more significant events. Elgar and Stravinsky were leading composers, though you might like to use the Beatles or other twentieth-century popular music. As we all know, this has been a time of immense technological development.

A simple and effective idea is to have an 'Enter/Exit Music' spot, illustrating a different composer for each century, with his details on your notice-board.

In common with all umbrella themes of the term, it is important to recapitulate as you go along, and most certainly at the end of the project.

DANCE OF THE WEEK

Dance of the week can be linked with other items in your class content. For example, if the Irish jig is the dance of one particular week, it could be linked with, say, dialect work contrasting the Irish brogue north and south of the border. There could be discussion work and situation drama on an Irish theme. Similarly, other dances will throw up important links to be used in the session.

Here is a list of popular dances that could be used:

> Zorba's Dance
> Irish jigs and reels
> The Hora (sometimes known as Hava Nagila, an Israeli folk
>   dance)
> Cha-cha-cha
> Rock 'n' Roll
> Ska
> Waltz
> Cancan
> The Polka

The Twist
Body popping
Break dancing
Disco dancing

Of course there are lots of folk and nationality dances you can add to your repertoire, such as the Gay Gordons and the Dashing White Sergeant. Dances through the ages, such as gavottes and minuets, could be an added dimension to your theme. The more specialized dances – such as tap, ballet, contemporary and modern – require years of discipline and training but, if you have someone in your class proficient in any of them, do have them demonstrate their skills. There is nothing to stop you, or the class, from choreographing your own dances.

Keep up with what's in vogue and remember the traditional dances too – and don't forget the Birdie Song!

AESOP'S FABLES

The sixth-century BC Greek slave Aesop told the most marvellously simple stories, mainly about animals. Each story has a moral and through discussion it is easy to find present-day parallels. The following ten have worked splendidly for us.

1   The Hare and the Tortoise

The hare is the faster runner but the tortoise wins the race because he is more persistent. Steady progress is better than a flash in the pan.

2   The Fox and the Crow

The fox flatters the crow about her voice; she opens her mouth to sing and drops the cheese. Never be taken in by flattery.

3   The Fox and the Grapes

The fox can't reach the bunch of grapes so he walks away in disgust saying, 'They were sour anyway.' It is 'sour grapes' to put down something you can't have.

4   The Lion and the Mouse

When the mighty lion is captured, it is the tiny mouse who gnaws through the ropes and releases him. Even the humblest creature is not beneath consideration.

5   *The Town Mouse and the Country Mouse*

The town mouse can't get used to the simple ways of the country
and the country mouse is frightened of the busy town. A case of
'One man's meat is another man's poison'.

6   *The Boy who Called Wolf*

After the shepherd boy has raised several false alarms, no one
believes him when the wolf really does attack his flock. People who
tell lies lose their credibility.

7   *The Dog and the Reflection*

A dog with a bone, seeing his reflection in a pool, tries to steal that
bone too, thus losing both. By being too greedy you can lose
everything.

8   *The Mice in Council*

The mice decide that a bell should be put on the cat so that it won't
be able to catch them; but who will bell the cat? It is easy to be an
armchair critic.

9   *The Dog in the Manger*

Although the dog can't eat hay himself, he lies on top of it and
makes sure the horse can't get any either. Don't deprive someone of
something just because you can't have it yourself.

10   *The Boys and the Frogs*

Throwing stones at the frogs may be fun for the boys, but it is a
matter of life and death for the frogs. Bullies should look at things
from the point of view of their victims.

Aesop's Fables can be dealt with dramatically in a variety of ways.
Divide the class into groups and allocate each group a different fable;
they have to devise a playlet re-enacting the original fable in modern
terms. An idea for individual work is for the class to hear one end of
a telephone conversation; at the end of it they must guess which
fable was being represented.

GREEK MYTHOLOGY

Greek mythology is important in all the arts. The myths have been preserved by the Greek poet Hesiod and by Homer in the *Iliad* and the *Odyssey*. The Greek dramatists of the fifth century BC – Aeschylus, Sophocles and Euripides – relied on myths and legends for most of their plots. Examples are *Medea* and *The Trojan Women* by Euripides. Throughout the ages playwrights have drawn on the Greek myths. Many of the terms have seeped into our language – *Achilles' heel*, your weak spot; *laurels*, the symbol of victory; *narcissistic*, intensely vain; *nectar*, the drink of the gods.

The Greek myths provide excellent material for storytelling, as well as improvisation and mime. Here are some that have proved very popular.

1   Pandora's Box

Pandora, the Eve of Greek mythology, was as beautiful as any goddess but she had a box which, when opened, loosed all the evils there are in the world, leaving behind only hope.

Thus woman gets the blame for all the evils in the world.

Spotlight Subject: 'Blame'   Getting the blame, whether deserved or not.

2   Demeter and Persephone

Persephone, daughter of Demeter, goddess of nature, was kidnapped and taken to the underworld. Zeus, chief of the gods, agreed to get her back but, as she had eaten six pomegranate seeds in the underworld, a compromise had to be reached by which she spent part of the year there and the remainder with her mother.

This is supposed to be the origin of the seasons.

Spotlight Subject: 'Compromise'   When two people disagree they can agree to differ or find a way of reaching a compromise.

3   King Midas and the Golden Touch

King Midas was granted a wish by the god Dionysus and he asked that everything he touched should turn to gold. Midas soon regretted his wish when even his food turned to gold. Dionysus bade Midas bathe in the River Pactolus, whereupon the golden touch passed into the waters, which flowed with gold ever after.

Today we talk of someone having the 'Midas touch', meaning that everything they turn their hand to is successful and makes money.

Spotlight Subject: 'Greed'   There is a difference between having a good appetite and being greedy. This applies to money as well as to food – and the greedy person always has to pay a price.

4   Daedalus and Icarus

Daedalus and his son Icarus were imprisoned in the labyrinth, a maze which he himself had built. They escaped by making wings from feathers held together by wax. Elated by the thrill of flying, Icarus ignored his father's advice and flew too near the sun. The wax melted and Icarus fell to his death.

Thus, Daedalus, the father of invention (he also devised the saw and the axe), saw his own son destroyed by his brainchild.

Spotlight Subject: 'Risk'   Nothing ventured, nothing gained – but beware the thrill of danger; risk-taking can become a compulsion.

5   The Stories of Perseus

Acrisius was warned by the oracle that his daughter Danae would have a son who would kill him, so he locked her up in a tower. But Zeus, chief of the gods, visited her there and fathered a son, Perseus, who grew up to have many adventures. Years later, when Acrisius was an old man, Perseus accidentally killed him when throwing the discus, so the prophecy came true.

Spotlight Subject: 'Fate'   Are certain things destined to happen or can people alter the inevitable course of events?

One of Perseus's adventures was when a king, Polydectes, wanted to marry Perseus's mother, Danae, against her will. Deceiving Perseus into thinking he was going to marry someone else, Polydectes sent him to cut off the head of the Gorgon Medusa as a wedding present. Medusa was so ugly that anyone looking at her turned to stone. Perseus cut off her head, but on his return he found Polydectes still pursuing Danae, so he showed him the head, turning him to stone.

Spotlight Subject: 'Deception'   If someone is deceived into doing something, the deceiver often gets his just deserts.

On his way home with the Gorgon's head, Perseus visited Ethiopia, where the queen, Cassiopeia, had claimed to be more beautiful than the sea nymphs, thus causing the land to be ravaged by a sea monster. The only solution was to sacrifice the king's daughter, Andromeda, to the monster by chaining her to a rock. Perseus killed the sea monster, rescued Andromeda and married her.

All the characters in this story are represented among the constellations of the autumn night sky.

Spotlight Subject: 'Sacrifice' Few worthwhile things can be achieved without sacrifices, but the sacrifices can sometimes be too severe.

6 *Orpheus and Eurydice*

Orpheus, son of Apollo, was such a wonderful musician that even the animals listened to him. He was married to Eurydice, but one day she was bitten by a snake in the grass and her spirit went to the underworld. Orpheus descended to the underworld after her, playing his lyre and charming the three-headed dog, Cerberus. Hades and Persephone agreed to release her, on condition that Orpheus would not look back at her, but just as they arrived at the gates he did and she disappeared for ever.

Spotlight Subject: 'Regret' It is no use trying to change the past but you can learn from it.

There are, of course, many more Greek myths and it is worthwhile to research them in both children's books and more academic ones. Improvisations can be built round the spotlight subjects and the myths lend themselves to re-enactment in modern terms.

BIBLE STORIES

The Bible is a great source of eminently suitable material for improvisation. Powerful storylines and themes of good versus evil make for strong dramatic content from which a moral can always be drawn.

Use 'This Week's Bible Story' as your umbrella theme in conjunction with 'Word of the Week' and 'First Lines'.

> Adam and Eve – 'temptation' – 'I told you not to do that'
> Cain and Abel – 'jealousy' – 'You're just jealous!'
> Noah's Ark – 'shelter' – 'You don't appreciate a thing I do'
> Tower of Babel – 'language' – 'No foul language in this house'
> Abraham – 'birth' – 'I'm pregnant'/'My girlfriend's pregnant'
> Isaac – 'sacrifice' – 'A little bit of self-sacrifice goes a long way'
> Jacob – 'deception' – 'How can you be so deceitful?'
> Joseph – 'dream' – 'Last night I had this incredible dream'
> Moses – 'rules' – 'You know the rules of this house'

And so on right through the Old and New Testaments.

BOOK OF THE WEEK

Theatre and literature walk hand in hand. There are all kinds of ways of bringing books into a drama class, from recommending favourite books or holiday reading suggestions to discussion work on books the class has read.

The book of the week can also be linked with a word of the week.

> *Gulliver's Travels* by Jonathan Swift (1667–1745) – 'travel'
> *The Happy Prince* by Oscar Wilde (1854–1900) – 'selfless'
> 'How the Whale got his Throat' from the *Just So Stories* by Rudyard Kipling (1865–1936) – 'enterprise'
> *Treasure Island* by Robert Louis Stevenson (1850–94) – 'pirate'
> *The Three Musketeers* by Alexandre Dumas (1802–70) – 'three'
> *The Hound of the Baskervilles* by Sir Arthur Conan Doyle (1859–1930) – 'eerie'
> *Around the World in Eighty Days* by Jules Verne (1828–1905) – 'time'
> *The Wind in the Willows* by Kenneth Grahame (1859–1932) – 'conceit'
> *Peter Pan* by J. M. Barrie (1860–1937) – 'age'
> *The Ugly Duckling* by Hans Christian Andersen (1805–75) – 'prejudice'

The word of the week need not be taken too literally. For example, when doing *Treasure Island*, the word 'pirate' could be connected with the pirating of ideas, video piracy, and so on. A simple word like 'three' (*The Three Musketeers*) can lead to such diverse topics as the eternal triangle; two's company, three's a crowd; St Patrick's illustration of the Holy Trinity using a shamrock; the three Rs; the three wise monkeys; and all the words beginning with tri–.

You can give the flavour of a book by reading apt extracts from it. It is very useful, particularly with juniors, to have your own fund of stories that you can tell in your own way. Plenty of raw material can be found in fables and fairy tales, let alone making up your own – however tall. A delightful tale to tell in your own words is the story of the Willow Pattern from ancient Chinese folklore – of course you must use the picture for illustration.

PERSON OF THE WEEK

'Person of the Week' can include all manner of prominent people –

artists, writers, composers, scientists, people in history, people in the news. Your choice of person can tie in with their date of birth or death or a centenary or a connection with something topical or newsworthy. Again, 'Person of the Week' works well with 'Word of the Week'.

> Thomas Hardy (1840–1928) – 'fate'
> George Orwell (1903–50) – 'satire'
> Mozart (1756–91) – 'talent'
> Mendelssohn (1809–47) – 'wedding'
> Charles Dickens (1812–70) – 'debt'
> Captain Cook (1728–79) – 'discoveries'
> Vincent Van Gogh (1853–90) – 'destructive'
> Sir Alexander Fleming (1881–1955) – 'health'
> St Patrick (*c.* 389–461) – 'confessions'
> Henrik Ibsen (1828–1906) – 'isolation'
> Queen Elizabeth I (1533–1603) – 'suspicion'

Obviously, we are not summing up a person's whole life in one word but rather homing in on one aspect and using it for dramatic purposes. Take Thomas Hardy. You would tell the class about his life and his works, perhaps read one of his poems, and describe Wessex and the typical names he uses for his characters. You could describe the role played by fate in his novels (you might, of course, have chosen a different word). Are members of the class fatalists or not? How much are people in control of their own destiny?

HEROES AND HEROINES

First introduce the topic by discussing the characteristics of heroism. What makes a hero or heroine? Perhaps they are the kind of people worthy of our admiration. What would you regard as heroic qualities? Courage? Daring? Great deeds? Contrast heroism and hype. Invite individuals to nominate a person they admire and say why.

Draw up a list of heroes and heroines from the past and present and choose a 'spotlight' word to home in on with a first line to follow.

The following list proved an effective one for us:

> Thomas à Becket (*c.* 1118–70) – 'resolute'
> 'No way. There is no way I'm going to change my mind.'
> Joan of Arc (1412–31) – 'messenger'
> 'Didn't you get my message?'
> 'What message?'

Horatio Nelson (1758–1845) – 'duty'
'Don't you have a sense of duty?'
Elizabeth Fry (1780–1845) – 'reform'
'You'd better buck up your ideas.'
Mary Seacole (1807–81) – 'prejudice'
'I'm sick to death of your prejudiced remarks.'
Martin Luther King (1929–68) – 'dream'
'Last night I had this really strange dream.'
Mahatma Gandhi (1869–1948) – 'truth'
'That was a bare-faced lie.'
Bob Marley (1945–81) – 'emancipation'
'Why do you allow yourself to be treated like that?'
Bob Geldof (born 1954) – 'generous spirit'
'Why can't you be more supportive?'
The Unknown Warrior (buried 1920 Westminster Abbey) –
'remembrance'
'You've got a short memory, haven't you?'
Mother Teresa of Calcutta (born 1910) – 'selflessness'
'Self, self, self. That's all you ever think of.'
Nelson Mandela (born 1918) – 'perseverance'
'I'll tell you something – you give in far too easily.'

The first-liners can be conveniently used in duologue form with
or without soliloquy – as you will.

Much mileage can also be gained from 'talkabout' duologues. For
example, with Elizabeth Fry and 'reform' the pairs cold talk about
areas of improvement personally and professionally. Or with
Mahatma Gandhi and 'truth' the class could play the game 'Tall Tales
or True'. The subject tells a tall tale and a true tale; the class has to
guess which was the tall one and which was the truth. This can also
be done in pairs.

Clearly some research will need to be done on the individual
heroes and heroines, but you will find that quite a few of the class
will gladly do some of this, so encourage optional homework!

A good ender on this topic is to pose the question to every
member of the group, 'Which hero/heroine meant the most to you
and why?'

A Heroes/Heroines Quiz might be another fun finish.

PLAYWRIGHT OF THE WEEK

This umbrella theme provides a useful 'in' to a writer's work. On your
notice-board have three headings:

PLAYWRIGHT OF THE WEEK

RECOMMENDED READING

THIS WEEK'S SUBJECT

Underneath these headings put your selections for the week. Hold a short discussion on the writer's life and work and the subject you have selected for improvisation. The following have worked well for us:

> George Bernard Shaw (1856–1950), *Pygmalion*, 'hypocrisy'
> Oscar Wilde (1854–1900), *The Importance of Being Earnest*, 'wit'
> John Osborne (born 1929), *Look Back in Anger*, 'grievance'
> Christopher Marlowe (1564–93), *Doctor Faustus*, 'debt'
> Arnold Wesker (born 1932), *Roots*, 'desertion'
> Harold Pinter (born 1930), *The Birthday Party*, 'unprovoked attack'
> Nigel Williams (born 1948), *Class Enemy*, 'language'
> Brian Clark (born 1932), *Whose Life Is It Anyway?*, 'choice'
> Tennessee Williams (1914–83), *A Streetcar Named Desire*, 'suffering'

The format for 'Playwright of the Week' is similar to 'Person of the Week'. Use of the subject need not be confined to its original meaning in the play – the group can branch out in any direction. For example, *Class Enemy* is a play with a great deal of swearing in it. You might mention that plays in the British theatre were censored by the Lord Chamberlain until 1968. How far is it justifiable to use bad language in a play or an improvisation? When does it become gratuitous and undermine the believability of the piece? You can then extend into foreign languages, dialects, accents and snobbery, sign language, malapropisms, slang, and so on.

OTHER THEMES

With older groups there is literally no limit to the themes that can be chosen for discussion and improvisation. Here are some suggestions taken from a series we did on contemporary topics: 'Snobbery', 'War', 'Religion', 'Sport', 'Power', 'Love', 'Animals', 'Alcohol', 'Defeat' and 'Rumour'. For example, 'Rumour' – stories that spread from person to person, but on a larger scale than gossip. It is hard to determine how rumours start but they can only spread if people, in some sense, want to believe them. Discuss how rumours start, spread and change. Why do certain people repeat (and embellish) rumours of particular kinds? Rumours tend to concern charismatic figures, fatal incidents, the supernatural, and high technology, and they are particularly common in wartime and other times of stress. See how many examples people can think of and then follow up with group work with the optional title 'The truth about . . .'.

It is a pity that the arts and sciences are so polarized. If you have some knowledge of science or a scientific colleague who is interested in theatre it is a field rich with possibilities. Just as we don't teach drama only to create actors and theatre audiences, similarly we don't teach science just to produce scientists, but to produce people with open minds who are willing to test theories by finding out the facts. Ground that can be covered includes opinions and attitudes to science, the dramatization of scientific ideas and the effects of scientific and technological developments. Science need not be confined to things that are done in a laboratory and a good 'talkabout' subject is 'One thing you've found out about, whether in a science lesson or not'. Another is 'One thing you wonder about – how something works, or why something is'. Improvisations can be based round situations where, for example, one invention is cancelled (for example, televisions either don't work or have never been invented) or one scientific law changes. Or, again, two people are given the responsibility of creating a new universe: what differences will they make from the one we have already got. A good topic for group plays is life fifty or a hundred years in the future. Start by looking back the same length of time and pointing out all that has changed.

Sometimes topics can be connected with particular styles of theatre. For example, a session on 'dreams' might connect with the Theatre of the Absurd, and perhaps you could go on to the Theatre of Cruelty, Surrealism and nonsense literature. One on 'journalism' or 'the media' might be linked with biographical theatre. Going back to playwrights, another way of working with older groups is to concentrate on the style and atmosphere of each writer's plays. Often a good 'way in' is to find a phrase that characterizes the writer, for example:

Samuel Beckett	Life and death in the wasteland.
Noel Coward	Exquisite wit. The characters often combine intensity and flippancy.
Mike Leigh	Caricatures of normality.
Joe Orton	Hilarious terror.
Harold Pinter	Extreme ordinariness – but with undercurrents of aggression and nothing completely explained.
Sheridan	Polished society comedy.
Tom Stoppard	Brilliant absurdity – confusions, parodies and jokes.
Oscar Wilde	Elegant high comedy.
Tennessee Williams	Decayed gentility – set in the Southern states of the USA.

Groups can even try to improvise in the style of a playwright they are studying, but, to be anything more than pastiche, such improvisations must be played very straight.

4

Short Productions and Drama Workshop Entertainments

It is always fascinating to be a 'fly on the wall' watching a good drama class in action, so it is not surprising that a drama workshop, presented to an audience, makes such a good form of entertainment. This requires a group who are technically proficient and confident enough to appear in front of an audience, and selection of the right material for the situation is important too. Professional improvisation groups have used a drama workshop format to good effect, and, particularly with unscripted intervention from the audience, this can be the liveliest form of live performance. You do have to be careful, though, to protect your performers to some extent: in a class you are used to producing an atmosphere in which people can experiment without the fear of failure; any failure in front of an audience is more likely to knock their confidence, so you cannot be so experimental.

THE TEN-MINUTE ASSEMBLY

A school class's first venture into drama workshop entertainment is likely to be a 'ten-minute assembly'. More than likely this will be tied to a topical subject or a date in the calendar — we've listed some later on — but our 'Umbrella Themes of the Term' (Chapter 3) should provide another fund of ideas to be narrated, mimed or improvised, such as Aesop's Fables, Greek mythology, the Bible, and so on.

Building up your own record and/or tape library is invaluable not only for mood and movement purposes but also because some musical narratives — for example, 'Tubby the Tuba' and Prokofiev's 'Peter and the Wolf' — lend themselves particularly well to a short entertainment.

Improvisations on topics currently being taught in class in such subjects as history and geography provide a good opportunity for a presentation to the rest of the school, and for sharing valuable information at the same time.

Take a history project, 'People Through the Ages'. There would be an endless list of people to choose from: St Patrick, Alfred the Great, Robert the Bruce, Sir Thomas More, Sir Walter Ralegh, Captain

Cook, Clive of India, Elizabeth Fry, David Livingstone, Florence Nightingale, Captain Scott, Lawrence of Arabia, Sir Alexander Fleming.

The narrator tells the story, possibly with mood music of the period topping and tailing his words. The main body of the piece can be mimed or improvised. Any extras such as costume, pictures or other material would be a bonus.

Children love a good story and assembly time is a good time to tell one. The story of Robert the Bruce and the Spider is a good example.

Robert the Bruce of Scotland was fighting a battle against King Edward of England. But Robert was feeling very downhearted as he was losing the battle. So he went down into a cave underneath the battlefield and laid himself down. As he lay there pondering he saw a spider weaving its web in a corner of the roof of the cave. But, every time the spider tried to weave the web, the web broke – again and again and again. But the spider did not give up hope, it went on trying again and again and again, until finally it succeeded in weaving the most beautiful web right across the roof of the cave. Robert the Bruce thought to himself, 'If at first you don't succeed, try, try, try again.' So he got himself up and on to the battlefield, fought the battle of his life – and became King of Scotland.

Another example is the story of St Patrick teaching the Irish people about the Holy Trinity. 'What do you mean, Patrick, by three in one? Do you mean three gods or one god?' Patrick bent down and plucked a shamrock from the Irish soil. 'Look,' he said, 'look at this shamrock. It's got three leaves but only one stem, three in one. God the Father, God the Son and God the Holy Ghost – three in one.' A large cardboard cut-out of an emerald-green shamrock would be a necessary visual aid to illustrate this.

A lot of material can be had from a project on 'Different Countries of the World'. Living in the multiracial society that we have today, we can find great pleasure and joy in sharing each other's cultures, from food to folk stories, from dialect to dance – in short, the way we live. For example, comparing a day in the life of an Israeli boy or girl with a day in the life of a Jamaican boy or girl – right down to eating matzos and roti – would be great fun.

In all these ideas, whether you're illustrating another school subject or not, it is vital to have strong dramatic content that will stand up in its own right, and even in a short production like this a good shape with a strong beginning and ending is essential. Do not over-rehearse the action – it is improvisation and you don't want to kill the spontaneity; but do give some attention to the practicalities — how are people going to get on and off the stage, where is an imaginary doorway going to be, which way are people going to be facing, etc? That way the actors are working in a secure framework. Audiences notice all the small details; one thing to try to avoid is a mixture of real and imaginary props, which looks false. Advise your actors, if they make a mistake, to stay in character and carry on as if nothing has gone wrong. It is not the mistakes that the audience notice so much as the actors' reaction to them.

OUTSIDE PERFORMANCES

The next step a class or club might take would be to perform a drama-workshop show in a children's library or a hospital or a pensioners' club. About a dozen is a good number. All the equipment you need can be put in one box or basket — some records, masks, a couple of telephones and a bell, a football rattle, a scarf, maybe two or three other special props or costumes you know you will need. Always make sure in advance that a record-player will be available and check what furniture you will be able to use and that the acting area and seating plan are all right.

Here is an example of a *Drama Workshop Entertainment* suitable for a library or adventure playground audience. The format could be made to work with any age-group from five to fifteen, but it is useful if you can find out the expected age range from the organizer in advance. It is also a good idea not to allow admission for under-fives. If the venue is one that you need to attract people to — a youth club, say — you can visit it a few evenings before to do some pre-publicity with its members (at the same time you can check the technical requirements are in order) and you can leave behind a poster:

DRAMA WORKSHOP ENTERTAINMENT

Come and watch — or, better still, join in!

Once the show begins you will be in charge of controlling the audience and bringing them into it as required. You will have some set pieces for your own performers and some items in which you will invite the audience to join in. It is usually easy to spot who is ready to come forward and you can gradually build up the amount and degree of audience participation.

The following programme may serve as a guide.

1

The masked dance is a good opener. Each member of your team wears a different mask. They come in one by one and freeze in appropriate postures. When they are all in, the tableau can be restarted and then frozen again for dramatic effect.

2

Mask characters provide another good set piece to follow. Take two popular mask characters — perhaps the baby and the ghost, or the boy and the gorilla, or the sailor and the blonde — and have two other people's disembodied voices talking for the two masked characters. Maybe the baby is frightened of the ghost — who happens to be the ghost of the library (or whatever) where you are working.

3

Hands improvisation — get your best talker to welcome the audience and introduce you as the leader of the group. While he (or she) is chatting away another of your team is standing right behind him with his arms through the speaker's armpits providing his 'hands' — with all the gestures (the speaker's arms go round behind both of them).

4

Enter yourself to welcome the audience and introduce the team.

5

The team members introduce themselves by giving their names plus, perhaps, the food they love to eat and the food they hate to eat.

6

You start the physical warm-up with the team plus members of the audience, if they are willing to join in. Some may prefer to watch — don't force them.

7

Voice warm-up, using tongue-twisters, four times after a count of two — 'good blood, bad blood', 'unique New York', 'red lolly, yellow lorry', 'bed spreaders spread beds but bread spreaders spread bread'.

8

The Inner and the Outer Circle (see Chapter 2), the team working with the audience.

9

Fact-finding — each member of the team has a partner from the audience and each has to find out at least five facts about the other in two minutes. Hear some of them.

10
Duologues – parents and children. The team play the parents. First line – 'You know the rules of this house.'

11
A mini-play (the audience go back to their places) – 'Divided Loyalties' (see Chapter 1), topped and tailed with music and with a *vox pop* from each character at the end.

12
Mime and music – the instruments of the orchestra. To suitable music the team and the audience together mime different musical instruments from the string, woodwind, brass and percussion families – not forgetting the conductor with his baton.

13
Story time – three props on a box. Select three props – say, a hairdryer, a vase of flowers and a pair of scissors (they can be virtually anything you happen to have). One of the team tells a story including all three props. Perhaps one of the audience is ready to tell a story too.

14
Bell stories. Your best storyteller sits on a stool and starts to tell a story. Every time you ring the bell he starts a new story (about four in all).

15
One-word stories. Each member of the team chooses someone from the audience and they act out a story as they tell it, each of them supplying alternate words starting with 'we' – 'were'. . . . Give an example or two from the team first.

16
Marching. One of the team leads the march, follow-my-leader style, and picks, one at a time, anyone who wants to join in.

17
Endgame – Adam and Eve. The students form a circle sitting cross-legged. Two of them are selected to be Adam and Eve and go into the middle. Adam is blindfolded and has to try to catch Eve, who has to stay within the circle. He calls out, as many times as he likes, 'Where are you, Eve?', and she must reply straight away, 'Here I

am, Adam.' Thirty seconds to catch her in and then, of course, Eve can chase Adam too.

18
The masked dance can be your finale, so that you finish as you started.

The above programme will take between 45 minutes and an hour, but always have spare material at hand and be prepared to cut when necessary.

As always, check your props list and record-player before and after the show. It is also advisable to appoint two stage managers from within the team.

THEME SHOWS

The next step is to put on a show for the rest of the school, or for parents and friends. A good idea is to build a show round a particular theme. If you have been using an umbrella theme, items for the show will spring naturally out of the class's work, and you will have something to aim towards throughout the term. Themes such as we have suggested in Chapter 3 — mottoes, proverbs, poems, quotations, nationality or period dances, Greek mythology, Bible stories, books — would all lend themselves readily to a theme show.

Another approach is to be topical. Throughout the year many ideas will present themselves to you simply by being seasonal. Here are some well known and not so well known dates that might provide a jumping-off point:

January	New Year Resolutions
February	Chinese New Year
14 February	Valentine's Day
March	Mothering Sunday
17 March	St Patrick's Day
Easter	The Jewish Passover
23 April	St George's Day and Shakespeare's birthday
1 May	May Day
24 June	Midsummer Day
15 July	St Swithin's Day (which is supposed to determine the weather for the next forty days)
6 August	Hiroshima Day

15 September	Battle of Britain Day
September	Harvest home
24 October	United Nations Day
31 October	Halloween
11 November	Armistice Day
30 November	St Andrew's Day
6 December	St Nicholas's Day (the patron saint of children)
25 December	Christmas Day

There are many more you could choose and there are reference books that list famous days, saints' days, centenaries, and so on. And of course you can do a show on 'The Four Seasons' at any time of the year, possibly using Vivaldi's music.

Other ideas we have used in the past have included:

Pop Dreams   A series of dreams in which pop records came to life.

Pictures of You   Slices of life – a children's eyes' view of parents, families and neighbours.

Mystery and Imagination   All manner of suspense and spookiness.

The Food Show   All about food from diets to cannibalism.

British Allsorts   About the many different kinds of people that make up the local community – West Indian, Irish, Greek, Turkish, African, cockney, etc.

Dear Aesop   Modern-day equivalents of Aesop's fables, alternating with the stories being told in their original form.

Children of the Rainbow   The rainbow and the colours that make it up.

The Rockney Rabbit   A tribute to the cockney singers Chas 'n' Dave, using their songs as a springboard for plot and characterization.

Tribute shows often work well and the class's taste buds might be whetted by anyone from Beethoven to Bowie.

Hallelujah!   A choir of forty plus singing gospel songs and all individually dressed in black and white.

Often the subject-matter will surface from whatever the class is currently into, be it comics or cosmetics, but, if you are stuck for a theme, open up a discussion or a talkabout and you are sure to get plenty of suggestions. If you're not sure how much mileage there is in an idea, you can make it the subject of a lesson in which the class divides into groups to devise improvisations connected with the subject that has been chosen. What you will be looking for is variety in content and mood and ideas with scope for development.

One way of organizing your theme show is to delegate specific research groups to work under various headings. So 'Children of the Rainbow' would have different groups finding out about the seven colours of the rainbow – red, orange, yellow, green, blue, indigo and violet. (You can remember the colours of the rainbow by the line 'Richard of York gave battle in vain'.) The red group would find out everything to do with red, from red London buses to red for danger, and the other six groups would each find out as much as they could about their colour, in the shape of bits of information, associations, improvisation, poems, songs and dances. Indigo could include the colour purple; violet has the flower and the girl's name. It is for the teacher to sew all the pieces together. The idea of God putting a rainbow in the sky as a promise to Noah and his family that he would never destroy the world again might top or tail the rainbow show.

Whatever method you use, you will have a period during which you are gathering and developing material. After a while you will be in a position to select the best of what you have, with an eye on the length of show required, and to construct a running order. The first thing to do is to find a beginning and an ending – something at the beginning that will gain the audience's attention and be an introduction to the whole theme of the show, and something at the end which will be a summation of all that has gone before. Then you need to find linking material – incidental music that can be used all the way through, or a narration or a motif or a storyline that can link all your different items. The items themselves must run in a logical order so that one thing leads to the next. If there can be a variation of light and shade so that a fast item follows a slow one, a comic one is set against a serious one, or a solo piece is followed by having the stage full of people, so much the better. Often practicalities such as set and costume changes will have to be taken into account.

At the devising stage, one of the advantages of a theme show is that you don't need to have the entire cast present at every rehearsal, as you can rehearse different items separately. Once you have a running order, though, the show will begin to knit together much better when you have all the cast together and are rehearsing 'from the top'. At this stage you can still make amendments and alterations, fit in extra sections and cut out items that aren't working. But in every show there comes a 'point of no return' where, however good the new idea may be, it is too late to implement it, and you will have to insist on 'no more changes'. Changes between the last dress rehearsal and the first performance are not advisable.

COMPILATION SHOWS

What if you want to have a show to work towards but don't have a ready-made theme, or have material you want to use that doesn't conform to any particular theme? Here you can use a looser structure – a compilation show. The only criterion then for including material is that the audience may find it enjoyable or meaningful. Nevertheless, you can still shape the whole show so that it becomes coherent: it could be 'A Day in the Life of the Drama Club', or a celebration of its anniversary. By adjusting the material a bit, you may be able to produce some sort of storyline out of seemingly unrelated items. It could be a 'Canterbury Tales' type of structure, in which a group of people each have their own story to tell, so each story becomes a 'play within the play'; or an 'Odyssey' type, in which the sections are a series of adventures happening to one or more characters; or it could have a chain structure, in which one character from each story connects to the next story, perhaps going round in a circle and back to the beginning. Or you can present the show like a variety show with your best stand-up comic as the MC.

FESTIVALS

Another idea is to hold a competitive festival. Our own Festival of Plays is held three times a year, at the end of each term, and unfailingly provides a most popular occasion to round off the term's work.

Throughout the term the members (from the age of eleven) put on their own improvised plays. They are given a virtual *carte blanche* as regards subject matter, casting, lighting, sound, music, and so on. Each director/writer/deviser (often a partnership) will have done some preparatory work in their own time on plot and characterization. On the day assigned for them to put on their play, they take out their cast plus sound and lighting people at the beginning of the lesson (after the warm-up) and take them to another area, where they rehearse for half an hour. They then put the play on for the rest of the class, after which we comment and mark the play, its direction and acting standard. There is a panel of four from the rest of the class who also comment and mark. The six plays with the highest marks are the entries for the end-of-term festival. Maximum length is about twenty minutes.

An adjudicator (usually a writer, director or producer) is invited to come along and give his comments and award the prizes. We supply four book tokens for the winning categories, normally 'Best Play', 'Most Original Play', 'Best Actor', 'Best Actress' – though sometimes the adjudicator suggests a different category such as 'Best Choice of Music'. The element of competition adds spice to the occasion but, as in the Olympics, the important thing is 'not winning but taking part'.

DRAMA IDEAS FROM OTHER SCHOOL SUBJECTS

Drama lends itself to use in a school in collaboration with teachers of other subjects, and not only the obvious ones, such as history, religious education and social studies. As mentioned in Chapter 3, science could be a fruitful area of co-operation, and we are also sure that the teaching of foreign languages could be helped by elements of dramatization.

The role of drama in this is illustrative: it 'brings things to life' as nothing else can. It is not a substitute but a supplement for other forms of teaching. It does not convey a great deal of factual information or explain complex causes and effects. And it is unlikely to give a balanced argument on a subject. What it can do is involve both participants and audience emotionally so that they can feel an experience intensely. For example, drama can do little to explain the causes of the First World War, but it can do something to help one to appreciate what it must have been like for the people who had to fight in it. Its ability to make us experience things as if at first hand, rather than at second hand, is what makes drama such a powerful teaching tool for other subjects.

5

Full-Scale Productions: The End-of-Term Play

The next thing you will want to do is to mount a full-scale production of a play. In some schools doing the end-of-term play is one of the duties that comes with the job. If it can be a focus of activity in the school so that, for example, everyone in one year is involved in the production in one role or another, so much the better. All are used to the best of their ability; it is a fine way of giving students a taste of responsibility and everyone will get a sense of achievement from the finished product.

There are not many plays in the repertoire suitable for a first production by children or young people – particularly if you want to do something in modern English with a large cast. So usually, by choice or necessity, you will have to create your own material. Here is a step-by-step guide to devising your own plays.

Starting-Point

First of all you have to find a point to work from. You may choose a theme such as those we have discussed in Chapter 4 – in fact a theme show can sometimes turn into a play, if all the parts of the show connect together. We once did one, 'Love Fifteen', with the theme of first love, which developed a single storyline which turned it into a play. Or you might choose a theatrical idea, a 'What if . . .?', such as Peter Shaffer uses in *Black Comedy*. What if the characters are in darkness when to the audience the stage is lit, and vice versa? Or you might pick on a promising improvisation and say: 'What happened before? What might happen afterwards? Who else might come into the story?' Each of these gives you a starting-point. The final play may bear little relation to what you start with – you can diverge as much as you like – but unless you start with something you will never get anywhere.

Devising

The next stage is to set your cast to gather ideas and produce raw material. Divide them into groups to work from the starting-point in different ways. Try out different things. Ask the 'what if' questions and be receptive to just the same sort of suggestions when they come from the cast. Improvise your way through a rough plot and discuss how it can be developed. One way to help build a consensus about the play is to improvise round the story – improvise scenes that wouldn't be in the play but help fill in the background. This is a collective creative process but the director must ultimately be the arbiter and editor.

Groundwork

At about this stage you will need to get some research done. Depending on the subject of the play, you may need either some factual information, or historical details or technical background. Even if the play is set in the future, you will need to decide what year it is set in, what has happened between now and then, and all about how the robots behave!

Getting a firm framework of this kind of detail helps everyone to believe in the reality of the play. Actors, especially professional actors, have to be magpies for information. They never know what part they may be going to play, so the more they know about the whole world from computers to cookery the better.

Characters

Now you need to know a bit more about your characters. An in-depth interview (see Chapter 1) with each of the main ones is a good idea, the whole cast being present. There has to be a certain amount of give and take on characters; they cannot be developed in isolation any more than real-life people develop in isolation. Once the background of a character has been developed, the key area to look at is how they react under stress.

Relationships

Characters do not exist in isolation so it is worth looking at each character in turn and their relationships with all the other characters they come across in the course of the play. In particular, how do the relationships develop and change and therefore how do the characters change?

Shape

As the plot begins to fall into place, the play develops its shape. You need a strong beginning and a satisfactory ending that is not anticlimactic. The turning-points must be well placed. Each character must be introduced to the audience. When the audience leaves, have all the questions that need answering been answered? Some scenes will need developing; others will need cutting. You may want to try out different things such as incidental music — something that will create the mood without describing the plot too literally.

Outline Script

At about this time you will be able to write down an outline script giving the scenes, the key lines, the plot points and the action, which you can give out to the cast. How much you continue scripting beyond this point is a matter of choice. If you do so, you may need to warn your cast that the scripted play is exactly the same play that they have been freely improvising up till then, otherwise the existence of the script can throw them and make them start reciting the lines woodenly. In a long and complicated play you probably do need to have a pretty full script for reference, and anyway it is good to keep a record. A word processor, if you have access to one, makes the job of continually redrafting much easier.

Planning

Of course, you must have had some kind of outline plan from the beginning, but now is the time to firm up all your arrangements. How many performances will there be? Fix the dates and times. How many rehearsals will you need? Err on the generous side and distribute a schedule. Be strict on punctuality; thirty people waiting ten minutes for a latecomer means that five hours of their time is wasted. Appoint stage managers early on: they need to be patient, intelligent, reliable and hard-working. Insist that everyone helps them by keeping props and costume tidy and putting things back in the right place.

If you haven't already got one, choose a title. If you've been using a working title, see if you can think of a better one for the show itself. If a set is going to be built, or anything else is to be made for you, this needs to be started early, so that there will be time to rehearse with it and make any alterations that prove necessary. Anything that you need to hire, buy or borrow must be obtained as early as possible as well. If you have a flexible seating plan work out the best arrangement and rehearse using the acting area which that gives you. You cannot of course sell more tickets than the number of seats you will have. If you're using copyright material, make sure that

any fees have been paid (approach the publisher for plays, the
Performing Right Society for music).

Rehearsals

The important thing when rehearsing now is to let the play run, in as
large sections as practical, so that it develops a life of its own. After
each run you can give notes and dissect any tricky points. For
example, you may often have to change a move to produce a better
visual effect or give the audience a better view of the action and it's
as well to 'walk through' something like this a couple of times to
make the change stick. It is a good idea to use costumes and props as
early as possible, so they become a natural part of the play; if they
are brought in at the last minute they are liable to cause problems. As
rehearsals go on one of the things that can happen is that the play
can lose its freshness; you need to make an effort to maintain the
moods and emotions of the play, just as if what is being enacted is
happening for the very first time.

There is so much to do in any production that the technical
people tend to get neglected. It is worth having a technical run – a
rehearsal that concentrates on lighting, sound and stage management
– to sort out any problems they may have. If there are set changes
you can nearly always speed them up by allocating individual tasks to
different people and making sure that the new stage furniture is
brought on before the old is taken off, which gives you your new set
much more quickly. Another tip for stage managers is never to carry
one thing balanced on top of another – particularly if it's a glass vase!
Don't forget to rehearse the bows which are, of course, part of the
show. Try to have your last dress rehearsal at the same time of day
as the performance and make every single detail of what people do
backstage, etc., exactly the same as what they will do on the first
night. That way they will be completely prepared. Then, twenty-four
hours rest and – you're on!

Production

Mounting a theatrical production is a bit like going to war –
fortunately, without the bombs and bullets. As the producer, it is
your responsibility to maintain morale, encourage the faint-hearted
and control the impetuous, to make sure communications are good, to
delegate responsibility but still ensure that the jobs get done, to keep
order when chaos threatens and to cope with a situation where there
never seems to be enough time to do all the things that need to be

done. The shared pressures and comradeship help build lasting respect and friendship and all in all it is a good training for life.

One of the keys to making things run smoothly is to write things down. Have your own job list of things to be done, add to it as new ones crop up, and check off the items as they are done. On production nights have on a clipboard your own check list of what you are going to do in the order in which you're going to do it, and make sure that everyone else with responsibility has one too. Otherwise, when you're under pressure things are bound to be forgotten and you'll have the additional pressure of trying to remember if you have forgotten anything. If you've got a good team your main tasks will be to check that everything is going smoothly and to help with any unexpected problems. It is worth having a cast list (with telephone numbers in case of non-arrivals) and checking it off as people arrive, making a point of having an individual word with everyone, which is very heartening for them.

It is also a good idea to have separate lists of 'borrowings' – anything that has been borrowed or hired which must go back to the owner after the show – and 'consumables' – any food eaten in the play and anything that has to be damaged and must therefore be brought in or made up anew for each performance. Lighting and sound will have their cue sheets and stage management (and wardrobe if you have a separate person looking after this) will have a list of props and costumes so that they can check that everything is in the right place. Immediately after the show, they must re-run the list to get everything back in place before people leave the building having forgotten that they've got vital hand props in their pockets.

Some people like to have understudies. It is certainly a good idea to have a designated understudy for a very large part but, somehow, Dr Theatre is a great physician and, touch wood, it is rare for people to be taken so ill at the last minute that they cannot go on. Having understudies all round is liable to make people confused so it is probably best just to have an idea in the back of your mind of what you would do for each possible combination of absences. Of course, having a cast of actors well used to improvisation makes replacements that much easier. The theatrical tradition is for everyone to be in the theatre by the 'half', 35 minutes before the curtain goes up; with youngsters it is probably better to make it an hour.

If you want photographs taken, it is best to do this at a dress rehearsal or even to have a special photocall. Everyone likes to have something to keep as a memento of a show and it is a nice professional touch to have pictures on display as the audience comes in. It also reduces the interruptions caused during a performance by flashbulbs. A nicely designed programme always adds something, and if you are working in a school the art department may help with this. Do not forget to acknowledge all the people who have helped in any way.

You may or may not be responsible for the front-of-house arrangements. In either case, you need to run through the exact sequences of events and signals to get the show started at the beginning or after an interval, and how it is going to end. Make sure that front-of-house helpers know your requirements about discouraging eating, drinking, smoking and photography in the audience and the admission of babies – not to mention pets.

Text Work

Much of the above applies equally if you are working from an already written text. As outlined in the Introduction, it pays to get the feel of the play through improvisation before learning the words and you can flesh out the characters through discussing and improvising round the story. If the play is written in a type of language unfamiliar to the cast, you need to do quite a lot of groundwork on the vocabulary, the figures of speech, and so on, so that they can begin to 'think in the language' – making it seem to become a natural mode of expression. Do not be afraid to cut or alter a play if you believe that by doing so the playwright's intentions will be better carried out in the circumstances.

Musicals

If you are putting on a musical, or any play with songs in it, the main problem is to avoid the music and the acting coexisting unhappily as two separate areas of the show. Right from the start people need to see their singing as an extension of their acting performance; they sing in character and believe every word of the song just as they mean every line of the script. If you are lucky enough to have the music specially written for you, or are writing it yourself, one problem you have to cope with is the 'unfamiliarity factor'. That is, a song does not have as great an effect on an audience if they are hearing it for the first time as it does if they are already familiar with it. Don't forget that you can use some songs that already exist, possibly with changes of lyrics, and always look for ways in which you can reprise a number or use the same melody more than once.

Production Notes: Do's and Don'ts

Half an hour before each performance, give the cast your notes, last-minute advice and encouragement and any comments arising from the previous performance. Here are some standard reminders:

Believability Believe in what you're doing and make it seem to the audience that what they are watching is real life happening for the very first time.

The Second Night Beware of second-night blasé-ness. Keep first-night freshness throughout each performance. Don't forget that it's a new audience who have not seen the show before.

Beware of second-night disappointment. On the first night the adrenalin is running and it seems almost a miracle that you get through the show at all; by the second night everyone's level of expectation has been raised and some of the excitement has gone; everyone is liable to think that the play hasn't gone so well.

Audiences Audiences vary. Keep the standard up in front of an apparently unresponsive audience. They may just be enjoying themselves quietly. Be prepared for people's laughter; keep concentration and don't laugh along with them. Don't try to go on speaking through a laugh; wait till it is dying down before continuing. Equally, never wait for a laugh if you are expecting one; it may never come.

Projection and clarity The back row should not have to strain to hear. The audience has a blanketing effect on the sound in a room so you have to speak more loudly than in rehearsal.

Mistakes If something goes wrong, improvise your way out of it and act as if it was intended to be that way all the time. The audience isn't to know that it wasn't. Never point out in any way that a mistake has happened.

Concentration Do not think about who is in the audience. Concentrate all the way through even when not speaking; listening is very important.

Quiet Insist on quiet backstage both before and during the performance. It's easy for this to be forgotten when people are excited and, apart from disturbing the audience and the other actors, it is a sure sign that people are not applying themselves to the job in hand.

Consideration Put props and costumes back neatly in the correct place. Help the stage managers.

No Surprises Do not try anything new in a performance without consulting the director. It might throw the other actors.

Last-Night Jokes   Don't. They are liable to spoil the show and it's cheating the audience.

GETTING IDEAS

Here are some lines of approach to finding ideas for plays.

1   *Find a Story that Already Exists*

We have already written about the possibilities of making modern-day equivalents of myths and fables. There is a wealth of material in fairy tales, literature, the Bible, Classical plays, novels and pantomime that you can borrow from, taking greater or lesser liberties with the plot. You can either follow the original story religiously, translating every detail into equivalent terms, or you can just preserve the core of the story and alter everything else round it, or you can use the original story as a jumping-off point and spin a new play entirely out of it. For example, *Romeo and Juliet* was much later reinterpreted in a musical version, *West Side Story*, but *Romeo and Juliet* itself, like practically all Shakespeare's plays, was based on an already existing story.   ⁻

2   *Start with a Subject*

As when developing a theme show, you can start with any subject under the sun and work characters and a story out of it. One idea is to have a dramatized-documentary approach and choose either a subject from history – the slave trade, the building of the railways, or what happened in the locality in the Second World War – or a subject of contemporary interest, possibly one inspired by a television programme or newspaper article. Get your cast to research the subject, if possible by eyewitness interviews. In order to make the thing live you need to see it through the experience of one family or set of people and you want a play that is a work of imagination rather than just a dry retelling of facts. You could do a complete local pageant seen through the eyes of one family in succeeding generations. After the past and the present, another rich field is the future. What social and technological changes will there be and what will be their effects on people's lives? Again, the important thing is to create believable characters and an involving story set against the futuristic background.

3 Choose a Crisis

Sudden death, a racial attack, a factory threatened with closure, people held hostage by terrorists, someone reaching breaking-point and being struck dumb – these events all provide suitable situations. The play consists of what leads up to the crisis, the crisis itself and the aftermath. A good example is *Gotcha* by Barrie Keeffe.

4 Take a Familiar Situation and Add an Extra Ingredient to It

The situation is one the audience will know and recognize – perhaps a school journey, or a wedding day, a school assembly, a funeral, or a teenage party. Everything builds up and we see all the everyday details we are expecting. Then ... something happens.

An apt illustration is *Barmitzvah Boy* by Jack Rosenthal: all preparations are busily made for the grand occasion, but then, at the crucial moment of the service, the hero turns on his heel and walks out. The 'something happens' factor should be an unexpected turning-point which catches the audience unawares.

5 Put some Characters in a Stressful Situation and See What Happens to Them

Start with a set of characters each with their faults and virtues; perhaps they are based on characters already developed by some of the cast. Build a play round what happens when they are put in a difficult situation. It could be an extreme one, such as the threat of nuclear war, or a more everyday one, such as a couple getting married very young, a divorce, disability, teenage rebellion.

William Golding's *Lord of the Flies* is an example – a story about a group of boys who are thrown together on an island: how they cope, who becomes leader of the pecking order and what happens to the standards of the civilization they have left behind.

6 Dream Up a Theatrical Device

What if all the characters are animals? Or creatures from outer space? The device could be something that makes the world of the play different from the real world, as in Lewis Carroll's *Alice Through the Looking Glass*, or something to do with the staging, such as having the cast on roller-skates in *Starlight Express*, or giving a character additional powers, like the Inspector in J. B. Priestley's *An Inspector Calls*, who knows the guilty secrets of all the members of a family.

7 Find an Allegory

Choose an ordinary situation which can represent something much bigger. A man lives for his garden but it is a perpetual battle against the weeds, while a succession of strange people wander in and out of it. The garden could represent the whole world. A journey could represent the journey through life. There are plenty of examples, from the parables to *Gulliver's Travels*.

8 Make More of a Pastiche

Many young people are expert at adopting the styles of films and television programmes, be it *Dallas*, *EastEnders* or *Frankenstein*. Take one of these genres and develop characters and a storyline faithful to the style of the original but separate from it. Make it more than just a send-up, played for laughs.

9 Find a Location

A location – the ladies' room, a kitchen, a library, a betting shop, a doctor's surgery, a beach, Moscow, Marseilles, heaven, hell, the Cairngorms, a launderette, a bank, a supermarket – anywhere in the world may provide a setting for a play. What characters would there be there? What happens to them?

10 Build on a Character

Take a character, or perhaps a pair of characters, either ones that have already been created by people in your cast or an idea you have for a character that one of them could portray. Develop the characters as far as you can so that you and the actors know them inside out. Then put them on the starting-line and let the story begin. If the characters are strong you will find them, as it were, spinning out their own story.

6

More Ideas

In the years since *100 + Ideas for Drama* appeared we have developed many more drama ideas. Here are some of them.

GAMES

Endgame is the title of one of Samuel Beckett's plays, the last moves in the game of chess and often the last item of an Anna Scher Theatre session. Physical games, mental games, old and new, traditional ones passed on with bits and pieces added or subtracted. A game brings people together at the end of a class and helps you to end on a positive high note. Games are also useful as icebreakers and as an interlude between more serious items.

Air Traffic Control

Lay out a 'landscape' of mountains, represented by chairs and blocks, and in the middle chalk a 'runway' about a metre wide. The 'air traffic controller' has to guide the 'pilot', who is blindfolded and has his arms outstretched as 'wings', on a designated route round various turning-points to land on the runway. He can only use the words 'left' (meaning 'start turning left'), 'right' ('start turning right') and 'straight' (meaning 'stop turning and go straight on'). The pilot goes at a slow walking pace and may not stop. Have two teams divided into pairs of 'controller' and 'pilot'. Each pair that lands safely without stopping or hitting a mountain scores a point.

Alternate Bumps and Statues

A variation on 'Musical Bumps' and 'Statues' in which the first time the music stops it's 'Bumps' and everyone has to go down on the ground – last one is out. The next time the music stops it's 'Statues' and everyone has to freeze – anyone moving is out. Anyone doing 'Bumps' when it should be 'Statues' and vice versa is out too.

Key on a String

You have two groups of six. Person no. 1 in each team is given a key which has a very long string tied to it. He puts the key down his clothes at his neck and out at his ankles and then passes it to no. 2. While no. 1 is still feeding the string through his own clothes, no. 2 has put the key down his or her clothes, and on to number three. The first team to get the key and string right through are the winners.

Thumper

The group sits cross-legged in a circle. Each person chooses a simple two-second mime to represent a different animal. For example, a rabbit is done by putting up your fingers behind your head to represent the rabbit's ears and wriggling your nose; for a goldfish you just open and close your mouth several times; and for an elephant you move your arm to represent the trunk. Go round the circle and have everyone announce his or her mime and demonstrate it. To start the game, everyone thunders their fists on their knees and shouts 'Thumper!' Then the first person performs his or her own mime, immediately following it with someone else's. The person whose mime has been done then has to repeat it, following it with someone else's mime again, and so on until someone hesitates, or makes a mistake, or does a mime incorrectly, or laughs while doing it, in which case he is out and names the person to restart the game.

As in all elimination games, either elimination can be by 'sudden death' or else contestants can be allowed two or three 'lives'.

President, President

Everyone sits cross-legged in a circle. The first person is 'President', the next 'Vice President', then 'Secretary', 'Treasurer', 'One', 'Two', 'Three', and so on. Teach them a rhythm of four claps: 'Together, knees, together, to the side'. When everyone can do this in time together the game starts, with the President saying to an eight-beat rhythm: 'President, President (clap, clap) Three, Three (clap, clap).' Three has to respond straight away: 'Three, Three (clap, clap), Secretary, Secretary (clap, clap).' The game continues until someone makes a mistake, breaks the rhythm or stops clapping. This player must then go down to the last number and everyone in between moves up one space and gets a new name or number. The object is to work your way up to President.

The Name Brain Game

Send two people out of the room. The rest of the class forms a circle and when the first person re-enters the teacher starts the class off calling out their *second* names, once round the circle, the first person repeating it back to them, which is a useful aid to memory. (If anyone hasn't got a second name, one can be invented.) The first person attempts to remember as many of the names as possible on one hearing. Then the second competitor is brought in and pitted against the first one. In a group whose members don't know each other, you can of course use first names. Variations: the class call out their favourite fruit, or door number, or what have you. A particularly funny version is 'The Pets' Name Brain Game', in which they give the kind of animal and the name of an imaginary pet – 'A goldfish called Rover', 'A hamster called Marilyn', and so on.

Survivor Word Tennis

This is a variation on 'Word Tennis' in which two people have to name items in a given category – colours, drinks, diseases, television programmes past and present, in fact any subject you like – until one of them cannot think of a new one within three seconds. In 'Survivor Word Tennis', all form a circle and are given the subject, which remains the same throughout the game. Start round the circle, and when people can't think of a new word they will be eliminated one by one. However long the game goes on, no repetitions are allowed. Last survivor is the winner. This is a particularly good way of sharing general knowledge of the theatre by using subjects such as 'Playwrights', 'Titles of Plays', 'Titles of Films', and so on. 'Playwrights' might start: 'Shakespeare', 'Sheridan', 'Shaw', 'Tom Stoppard', which is easy enough – but it quite soon gets difficult!

Deliberate Mistakes

Read out a news item or tell a story and from time to time make a deliberate mistake. The first person to raise a hand gets a chance to correct the mistake and score a point for his or her team.

Incidentally, if you want a class to concentrate on the details of something you are telling them, it is quite a good trick to warn them that you are going to slip in a deliberate mistake you want them to spot.

Christmas Presents

Everyone sits in a circle. You start by saying: 'I'm giving Sally a sausage – she'd like that.' Sally must continue: 'I'm giving Martin a video.' 'No,' you cut in, 'he wouldn't like that.' Martin continues: 'I'm giving Chris a car.' 'Yes, he'd like that.' The presents they would like are the ones beginning with the same letters as their names. You have not told them this but as soon as they work it out for themselves they know what presents to give other people and can join in the chorus of 'He'd like that' or 'She wouldn't like that' until everyone has worked out the rule. The more comical the presents are the better. Every time you play the game you can use a different rule: they will only like the present if it begins with the *last* letter of the person's name, or the first letter of the name of the person sitting on their left, or it must be something they're wearing, or maybe they'll only like the present if the person giving it is sitting with legs crossed, or hands clasped, or touches his or her face before speaking.

Five Question Quiz

This is a useful mental recap game for revising the content of your previous lessons. It can take the form of, say, a Shakespearian quiz or a drama vocabulary quiz. Quickfire on-the-spot questions asked in sets of five to individuals dotted round the room provide a nice five-minute ender to the class. For example:

> Name William Shakespeare's wife.
> What date was he born?
> Who were the star-crossed lovers?
> What was the name of the most famous Elizabethan theatre?
> Where was Shakespeare born and where did he die?
> (Answers: Anne Hathaway; 23 April; *Romeo and Juliet*; the
>   Globe; Stratford-upon-Avon.)

Demonstrate a Game

This is a group-work idea that is also a useful way of building up your repertoire of games. Divide the class into groups, who each choose a game they want to demonstrate and rehearse how they're going to show it. Then each group shows the class in turn, the leader announcing the name of the game and explaining the object and the rules. Finally, the whole group demonstrates how it's played.

SPEAKEASY/TALKING POINT/TALKABOUT

Three names for the same basic idea. Put a seat centre stage as the 'hot seat', announce the subject, and one by one people come up and talk about it. Here are some topics:

> What gives me confidence
> Choose a name for a baby girl and boy and explain your choice
> One thing I regret and why . . .
> My ideal holiday
> Manners. Start off with 'I think it's good/bad manners to . . .'
> April Fool's Day
> Qualities in a friend
> Who I trust and why
> The best piece of advice I've ever had . . .
> The good/bad thing about being old
> New experiences in the last year; talk about the first time you did something
> Something I'll never forget
> What I'd do on a free day without money
> Who I'd like to be with on a desert island and why
> Saturday jobs
> Jobs I do around the house
> My idea of luxury . . .
> What I like to eat and drink in hot weather
> All the food I eat in an average day
> If I were my own parent . . .
> My idea of heaven on earth; my idea of hell on earth
> A place I'd like to revisit
> My Walter Mitty existence
> What frightens you
> My personal protest
> What I do to lift my spirits when I'm down in the dumps
> Superstition
> Dreams and nightmares
> My most treasured possession
> The book I'd recommend and why
> Fancy-dress ideas
> My weekend
> My bedroom
> Nicknames
> A club I belong to
> My experience in hospital
> What I'd do if I were unemployed

A tip for well-being – something that makes me feel good
The best/worst thing about the twentieth century
I'm an optimist/pessimist because ...
At the end of your life, what would you like to have
   achieved?

DISCUSSION

Here are some ideas for your class to discuss. You are the one to
control the proceedings by using hand signals and keeping it 'in the
middle'. Top and tail it with your preparatory work.

Phobias
Problems and solving them
Insults and compliments
Success and failure
How we treat old people
Accents and dialects
Afterlife
Home truths
Neighbours
Guilt
Bad language
Spring cleaning
Mob mentality
Prejudice
Secrets
Crazes, catchwords, catchphrases
Health
Temptation
Appreciation
Sacrifice
Deception
Rules
Choice

MORE TALKING HEADS

Divide the class into twos and threes. Set them a talking-piece and
the room becomes a sea of talking heads. After a minute stop them
and select people to summarize to the class what they've been saying.
Here's some examples.

Likes and dislikes in your family

On the subject of breakfasts ...

Full names of you and all the family

Favourite and unfavourite shops

Favourite things (pudding, member of the royal family, flower, TV personality, magazine or comic, etc.)

Describe how to prepare a TV snack.

Your 'moan of the moment'

Be your own critic – comment on a recent book you have read, or film or play you have seen

All about you (name, family, school, including best and worst subjects, hobbies and the job you'd like to do when you leave school)

STORIES

Bean Bag Stories

This is a storytelling game in which everyone stands in a circle. You start a story, holding a bean bag. After a couple of sentences you stop in mid-flow and throw the bean bag to someone else, who must continue the story from where you left off. Anyone who hesitates, can't continue, drops the bean bag or throws it unfairly is eliminated, or else perhaps loses a life and has to catch one-handed. The next person starts a new story.

Five-Minute Stories

A good ender, before the bell, for junior classes especially, is the five-minute story. Some people are natural storytellers and telling a story probably is preferable to reading it, but either way keep a record of those that work well. Your stock of stories will be very much a personal matter but bring in as much variety as you can. The local library is generally very helpful in selecting popular choices from the different categories. Firm favourites such as 'Perseus and the Gorgon Medusa' and the story of Icarus from the world of Greek mythology, 'The Boy who Called Wolf' and 'The Town Mouse and the Country Mouse' from Aesop's Fables, 'Fin McCoul' and 'Cucullin and the Children of Lir' from Irish folk tales, 'The Emperor's New Clothes' and 'The Little Match Girl' by Hans Christian Andersen, and *One Hundred and One Dalmatians* by Dodie Smith can hardly fail to go down well but a lot will depend on whether they are told expressively and with good characterization. Apart from general categories — adventure, fairy, folk, Bible, history — the teacher can always make up his or her own. A good ghost story will almost always go down a treat.

At the same time, keep a collection of favourite poems. Hilaire Belloc's *Cautionary Tales* would make an excellent starter.

MIME AND MOVEMENT

Hand-Sign Duologues

See how many hand signs the class can think of. Thumbs up, fingers crossed, waving, beckoning, blowing a kiss — there are dozens of them. Does anyone know any gestures used in different cultures and what they mean? Ask the class to divide into pairs and work out some hand sign duologues together — that is, whole conversations in hand signs only, including rude ones if necessary. Then see them all, two by two.

Silent Action

This is not strictly a mime idea but rather an exercise in acting without words. Two people are to act a duologue, the characters and situation being up to them (give them a moment or two to consult), but the keynote of the scene is given by you, and it must start with at least thirty seconds of silent action in that vein before the first word is spoken. For example, you could say that the scene should start with thirty seconds of silent fancying by one of the two people, or thirty seconds of silent mutual antagonism. Other possibilities are:

> Pleading for forgiveness
> Irritation
> Gloating
> Imagining the other in a different situation from the one he or she is in
> Thinking about something miles away from what the other person thinks you should be thinking about
> Thinking about something you've planned but the other person doesn't know about
> Eating.

This is a good exercise in the use of body language and

appreciation of the spaces between words. It is interesting how silent action always holds an audience's attention.

Tableaux

This is a piece of group work that is especially good for juniors. A tableau is an abstract picture formed by the bodies of a group of people, standing, sitting, kneeling or lying in any position. To suitable background music each group makes its own individual tableau, both dramatic and acrobatic. Symmetry can be added to the brief as an optional extra. After preparation time see them one by one, giving marks out of ten for originality and presentation, if you wish.

Improvised Dance Circle

This is a good warm-up idea. The class forms a circle and to some suitable music you start a repetitive dance step which they have to follow. Then call someone into the middle of the circle who has to start a new step, which everyone picks up and follows. Then someone else takes the lead and on the changeover the class keeps up a simple step or clapping pattern to maintain the rhythm.

A variation on this is for everyone to work in pairs and devise a simple routine in which one follows in mirror image steps devised by the other and vice versa. Each of the pairs can then demonstrate in the dance circle. This simple choreography can be a good shared experience. A further development is for one of each pair to improvise a 'question step' and the other to do an 'answer step' in response to it. These can then be picked up in pairs round the circle.

CHARACTERS AND PROPS

Here are some more simple ideas which help to develop the ability to adopt and hold a character.

Complaints

Everyone has to complain from time to time about something. Some people positively enjoy doing so. In 'Complaints' we have one side of a complaint to an imaginary person in which the complainer adopts whatever character he or she wishes. The setting can be a shop, a restaurant, an office, or anywhere else. The complaint can be about anything at all, whether it's important or trivial, and the person can be polite or rude, vague or precise, personal or impersonal, depending on the kind of character chosen. You will get plenty of material for discussion about the most effective way of getting your point across without putting the other person's back up, whether you're complaining or being complained to. A variation is the 'Chain complaint', like the 'Chain argument' in Chapter 1.

Parent, Neighbour and Teacher

This is another idea that combines character work with seeing things from other people's point of view. Ask the class to think of an imaginary parent, an imaginary neighbour and an imaginary teacher. What do each of them think of you, the child? Ask them to try to sum it up in a sentence or two. Then hear some of them. 'The parent?' you ask, and the parent's point of view is heard. 'The neighbour?', and we hear it from the neighbour's point of view. 'And the teacher?', and the teacher's point of view is heard.

Bell Characters

This is like 'bell stories', in which every time the bell rings the storyteller has to start a new story. Someone sits in the hot seat and every time the bell rings he or she has to adopt a new character and give us a snatch of his conversation, either talking to himself or to an imaginary other person, continuing until, after about half a minute, the bell rings again. Four or five characters is a good number for one person, and the object is to make them both varied and believable. You can try it out with the class working *en masse* first of all, before putting anyone on the spot.

Compelling Conversations

If you have a stock of telephones you'll need them all for this; otherwise they can be mimed. Have half a dozen people working together, each of them talking to an imaginary person on the phone. The brief is that they must be *compelling conversations*, the sort that, if you got a crossed line and overheard them, would mean you just couldn't put the receiver down before the end. Everyone does it together and then you hear them one by one.

Status Scenes

Because of their personality or position (for example, officers and men in the Army) some people adopt high-status, and some people low-status behaviour. Some of the indicators of high status are obvious – standing up straight, holding eye contact as opposed to furtive glances – but some are more subtle. The brief for this piece of work is that one character should be of high status, the other of low status. High-status always asserts himself and low-status defers, but in a subtle way. Then you can have two high-status people trying to outdo each other, or two people trying to play lower than each other. Try the latter with a couple chosen for each other by computer dating. As they each try to abase themselves to the other they become more and more lovable.

SITUATION DRAMA

Windows

This is a quick situation drama idea in which the whole class works at the same time. Give them a broad brief: they are in family situations, or a situation where someone is worried, or giving or receiving good or bad news. They are to work individually, talking to an imaginary person. After everybody has worked together you can hear a brief excerpt of some of them, just as if you were opening a window, overhearing some of the conversation going on inside, and then closing it again. Use 'action' and 'cut' to direct them. This is a good 'acting warm-up' idea to follow the warm-up at the start of a session and can be done in duologue form as well as monologue.

Rescue from the Railway Line

This is a high-energy piece. Someone has fallen on to a railway line. He may be trapped or unconscious. A train may come at any moment. Two other people see what has happened. They have to climb down to the track, avoid the live rails, and pull the person clear before the train comes. Maybe they will succeed, maybe they won't.

Monologue *en masse*

The boys and girls sit on the ground while you give them the brief. Then the class does a monologue *en masse* – that it, the whole group works individually but at the same time. After about half a minute to a minute you call out 'Cut'; all sit down where they are and you spotlight various members of the group in turn.

Letters

'You receive a letter which either contains good news or bad news. It could be from your aunt who's just had a baby. It could be from a friend inviting you to go on holiday with him or her. Your cousin has had an accident. You have won a prize in a competition. Your grandad has died. Your library books are overdue. Good news or bad news. Start the letter with "Dear ..." and your name. Stand up everybody and – Action!'

Locked in a Room

'You are in your bedroom reading. You happen to go to the door only to find that it is locked. You're puzzled. Is your brother playing a trick? Or is there something the matter with the lock? Or is there some more sinister explanation? Whichever, your slight annoyance builds up to a climax. You might even be a little bit claustrophobic. Let's start with you reading on your bed – Action!'

This idea could also take place in a lift.

Shock

'Who's good at screaming? Now's your chance! I'd like to start this improvisation with a little bit of mime. You are ironing a shirt. Or you might be changing the plug on an electric kettle. Or someone has unexpectedly slapped you on the back rather too hard. Whatever – you get a nasty shock. I'll give you a countdown of ten seconds – and then you scream. We see your reaction to the nasty shock – and then the aftermath. Are you shaken, angry, calm, tearful? Are you injured? How soon do you recover your composure? Ten, nine, eight ...'

Problems – Psychosomatic or Otherwise

The class can find a space with their chairs for this piece.

'You are at the doctor's. You've got a problem. It might be an emotional one – your mum is very depressed. It might be purely physical – you have an ingrowing toe-nail. It might be that you want to tell the doctor something that you feel is highly confidential. I shall start off as the voice of the doctor and then you, the patient, carry on talking to the imaginary doctor. "What seems to be the problem?"'

Lost and Found

'You've lost something very important to you – it could be a signet ring, a £5 note, an exercise book. You're hunting everywhere for it. I want to see a growing frustration as the tension mounts, until you find it. We'll start with the realization that the such-and-such object isn't where you thought you'd find it. You might start with "Where have I put my exercise book?" Think for a moment, and – Action!'

You can preface this with preliminary discussion on 'things you've lost and things you've found'. There will be much room for development work in twos and threes, and plays to follow on from the monologue.

The Eavesdropper

'Nobody likes being talked about behind his back – though Oscar Wilde said, "There's only one thing worse than being talked about – not being talked about." That may be so, but most of us are pretty sensitive about what is said about us. You overhear a so-called friend of yours backbiting about you like nobody's business. You *eavesdrop* and, while you know eavesdroppers never hear well of themselves, you are transfixed. You get angrier and angrier till you let rip on your imaginary friend. Let's hear you give him his come-uppance. Maybe a good first line might be "How dare you talk about me behind my back!" And action!'

Caution

'Never talk down to people – whether to under-fives or over-fives. Let's see you do this exercise in two different ways – two interpretations – once in anger, and the second time affectionately. You are warning a child about road safety. An optional first line is "Always stop, look and listen when you cross the road". The first time you are angry – perhaps the child ran into the road after a ball, without heeding the Green Cross Code. Action!'

Jealousy

'Shakespeare calls jealousy "the green-eyed monster". It is a horrible feeling. Your boyfriend or girlfriend has been seeing someone else without your knowledge. You are being two-timed. You feel betrayed. You have it out with them. . . .'

This is an interesting exercise to see from the other point of view.

Everyone has the right of reply. What has the 'betrayer' got to say? The follow-up can provide some good strong stuff.

Showdown

'What is your "moan of the moment"? Maybe it's the neighbour's saxophone which for some reason he seems to prefer to practise after eleven at night. Maybe it's a pneumatic drill in the street outside. Maybe it's a friend of yours who's always on about the Arsenal — and you can't stand them. Maybe it's your brother always wanting to watch *Top of the Pops* when you want to watch the other side. Whatever the cause of your displeasure, now is your chance to get it off your chest. Here's your chance of a grand showdown. First line — "I've had it up to here with you." Action!'

Bee in Your Bonnet

Another monologue *en masse*. Everybody has something they're a little bit obsessive about — some people have more than one. It may be smoke from other people's cigarettes, dogs that foul the pavements, having to queue to buy a train ticket, food with artificial preservatives in it. Whatever it is, it's something that causes annoyance out of all proportion to its importance. Hear people sounding off about a pet hate — it could be their own real life pet hate, or someone else's.

Political Point of View

'You hold a political point of view that you want to air. It can be big politics or small politics or some moral issue. You sound off about something that you feel strongly about. It might be vegetarianism. It might be vivisection, troops in or out of Northern Ireland, the monarchy — for or against, socialism, Thatcherism, homosexuality, school dinners, school uniforms — whatever. You sound off about it from *your* viewpoint. First line — "Listen to me for a minute will you?" Action!

Immediately after this exercise follow it up with the same person arguing the case from the opposite point of view. This is much harder. If the player would convince an outsider that he holds the opposite point of view to the one he really does hold, then he has succeeded.

Opposite Point of View

'We've heard your views on various social issues. Now I want you to put the case forward from an opposite point of view to your own.

This is much more difficult. Marshal your facts carefully. Fight with reason as well as emotion. You don't want to be high on emotion and low on logic. Keep it balanced; don't send it up. First line — "Now you listen to me!" Action!'

First Thing in the Morning

'It's 7 a.m. and it's time to get up for school. You are very reluctant to leave the shelter of the warm blankets. "Only five minutes more," you plead. I want to see it from your mum's point of view first and then from yours. First we'll hear your mum, and her first line is "Get up out of that bed, *immediately!*" Action!

'... cut! And now we'll see it from your point of view, in prostrate position. Lie down everyone. "Only five minutes more." Action!'

Urgent Message

'You've got to deliver an urgent message. Your mother has just been admitted to hospital, your little brother has just swallowed some tablets, or your friend has fallen and fractured her arm. You quickly pass the message on — "I've got an urgent message for you." Action!'

This exercise is most effective when you spotlight people individually, giving them the further direction of, say, ten seconds of running from point A to point B before delivering the message. The physical action heightens the urgency.

Shoot First and Ask Questions Afterwards

'Shoot first and ask questions afterwards. Have you ever had a real go at someone only to find that they were completely blameless? We all do it occasionally and often feel bad because of it. You make a verbal attack on someone. Maybe you accuse your best friend of trying to steal your boyfriend when in fact there's a perfectly innocent explanation for their being seen together. I leave the reason up to you, but, whatever it is, you're barking up the wrong tree. Off you go!'

This is a good piece to see from the other point of view as well.

The Apology

'Saying sorry isn't always easy. But a genuine sincere apology can often make the world of difference to a relationship when someone has been in the wrong. And, equally, it's important for the other person to forgive. OK. An apology is in order. And smirks or sniggers are not counted as a *sincere* apology. "I really am very sorry about last night." Action!'

Emotions

Another monologue *en masse* piece. The monologue must have a controlling emotion – anger, fear, hate, love, envy, depression, elation. It is interesting how the vocal tone of the whole class varies with the emotion.

Duologues

A Problem Shared is a Problem Halved

'You've heard the saying "a problem shared is a problem halved". Well, one of you has got a highly confidential problem – your parents are getting divorced and you don't know how to handle it; or you've failed an important exam; or you've put on a stone in the last month. You are rather desperate. You tell your best friend. The first line is "I've got a problem." Action!'

This is a good exercise for listening and also for giving advice. Discussion on problems and how to solve them is useful either before or after the duologues.

Something Personal

'You are very fond of your best friend – and rather protective towards him or her. But there is something he ought to know, something he is not aware of. And, though it's a bit embarrassing to say it, you'd rather that it came from you than have him the laughing-stock of the class. Maybe he smells. Maybe he's overweight, or spotty. You start by using his name – "John, there's something I've got to tell you." Action!'

Confessions

'Confessions are something Catholics will be familiar with; they confess to the priest something they have done which was wrong. You have done something wrong and are feeling rather guilty about it. You decide to come clean and say it right away to your friend. "Mary (or whatever name), I've got a confession to make to you." Action!'

Insults and Compliments

'In pairs, I want you to do two short and separate pieces – one in which one of you insults the other, and one in which you pay him or her a compliment. You will find that *dramatically* the one on "insults" will be a lot easier to do because of the element of conflict – and drama is conflict. Make the compliments genuine, not sarcastic ones. Don't forget to be gracious in your thank-yous on receiving a compliment – but let's start with the insults. Off you go!'

Whispers in the Library

'You are best friends and you have your first row. But it takes place in a library! So you conduct your row in whispers. There is an imaginary librarian present at a desk at the front. Here's an optional first line – "May I have the £5 I lent you back?" Second line – "I'm very sorry but ..." In whispers – action!'

Parental Displeasure

'Let's have a parent and a child. The child has incurred the parent's displeasure in some way – and now you've got to face the music. Nobody particularly likes criticism but the onslaught that you are going to get from your mum or dad is certainly something to dread. What the situation is, is up to you. Maybe you've had some tattoos done on your arm. Maybe your parents can't stand your punk boyfriend. Maybe you've gone a brassy shade of blonde. Whatever, Mum – or Dad – is raging. Action!'

Ending a Relationship

'"Parting is such sweet sorrow," says Shakespeare – but, let's face it, none of us likes to be packed in! Michael, you've been going out with Sarah for three months now. She's a nice girl but there are plenty of other fish in the sea. You do the proper thing and say it to her face – not by phone or by note. I want no cowards in my class! Here's an optional first line – "Sarah, I'm sorry, it's over." Now, that could be said kindly or harshly, and Sarah's reaction could be shocked or heartbroken, or she may try to hold on to the relationship, or she may lash out angrily. That is up to you. Action!'

It could be any relationship – boy and girl, homosexual, mother and son, partners in business. Put the class in pairs to work out a relationship and why and how it might be ended.

Private

'You are either two sisters, two brothers or a brother and a sister. And while you obviously share lots of things there are some things which are private. Your diary is one of them. On this occasion one of you comes into your bedroom and sees the other doing the unforgivable – reading your diary. Let's first see your reaction – the one reading the diary is oblivious to your presence. First line, delivered in a quiet tone – "You have no business reading *my* diary." Action!'

This works particularly well if one of the pair has the diary – or letter, or photograph, or whatever – physically in his or her hand and the other tries to snatch it away.

The Sack

'Nobody ever likes to get the sack. The humiliation is often too much to bear for the person being sacked but it's none too pleasant to be the bringer of bad news either. The situation may be that you are employer and employee, or axing someone from a band, sending someone down from college, or telling someone he is no longer required for the team. Do not be afraid to grasp the nettle. An optional first line might be "Sit down! I'm afraid I've got some bad news for you." Action!'

Accident

'Have you ever accidentally broken one of the family's treasured pieces – Mum's priceless Waterford glass vase, say, or Dad's ship-in-a-bottle? The guilt can be crippling. How can you make it up to them? You are doing your Saturday morning chores when the unforeseen occurs – the wretched thing slips to the ground and is shattered into smithereens. Come clean straight away. The first line is "Mum, I'm afraid I've just broken your Waterford glass vase," or "Dad, I'm afraid I've just broken your ship-in-a-bottle." Good luck! And action!'

The Borrowed Book

'When you borrow things you simply must return them in as good a condition as when you borrowed them. It's unforgivable to do otherwise. Sylvia, you've borrowed Marcia's book, *The Secret Diary of Adrian Mole (Aged 13¾)* by Sue Townsend. Sylvia, you return the book to Marcia – *in a deplorable condition.* The cover is torn, you've used chewing gum as a bookmark – it's quite disgusting. And to top it all you are quite unaware of the state the book is now in. Start with "Thanks for lending me your book, Marcia." Action!'

Requests

'There's a right way and a wrong way of doing everything, and if you're asking for something, whether it's a favour or something you have a right to, there's a world of difference between asking for it politely and asking for it rudely. There is also a world of difference in the response you're likely to get. Choosing the right moment is important as well. So I want two versions of the same duologue. Each time the same thing is being requested, but in version one it's being asked for in the wrong way, and in version two in the right way. Of course, politeness should not be confused with timidity, and it's possible to assert yourself without being rude. Action!'

The Last Straw

'In twos – you may be two friends, two sisters, mother and daughter, father and son, whatever. We see you at the climax of some sort of trauma: things have got worse and worse and now you are at breaking-point. You have one minute to either make it up or break it up! First line – "Look, this really is the last straw!" Action!'

Coping with a Temper Tantrum

'It's one thing to get angry; it's another thing to lose your temper. In a temper tantrum the person has lost his or her temper and is right out of control. In this duologue, just such a temper tantrum is bursting out and the other person has to do his best to cope with it, calm the person down and not provoke him to fresh anger. Or perhaps the second person argues back, or winds up the first even further – in which case the quarrel may escalate to who knows where.'

Unrequited Love

'It's awful when you love someone but they do not love you in return. Bernadette, you have fancied Robert for I don't know how long and now here's your chance. You're in the launderette watching the washing go round and round when who should come in with his washing but the man himself. He puts his washing into the machine but does not know how to work it. Bernadette, you're a dab hand at working the washing-machines in the launderette – you've done it every week since you were nine! Robert, you like this helpful girl but you are very much in love with your own girlfriend, Dulice. Bernadette makes her attraction to Robert pretty obvious. What is Robert's reaction? Is it "I like you but ..." or is it a direct put-down? And what is Bernadette's reaction to that? Her first line is "Can I give you a hand?" Action!'

The Last Bus Gone

Two people have gone out for the evening. They have to catch the last bus in order to get home. They have stayed a little late. It's cutting it a bit fine, but the bus will probably not be on time. They hurry round the corner to the bus-stop, only to see the back of the bus disappearing into the distance. What on earth are they going to do now? They only have the money for their bus fare. What is the safest thing to do? What will get them home most quickly? What are their parents going to say?

Schadenfreude

Schadenfreude – German for delight in someone else's downfall. Not a very pleasant reaction. Gail and Sanna, you've got my full permission to go as far as you like with this improvisation! Sabrina, the class snob, has just failed to get into drama school – or so you've heard through the grapevine. Sanna, we'll give you the first line – "Have you heard, Sabrina didn't get into drama school?" Action!'

Squeamishness

'If you can't stand the sight of blood this is a good one for you! It's about being squeamish. One of you is in some kind of pain – perhaps you've cut your finger with the carving knife, got a speck of dust in your eye, got really bad stomach ache. You go to your friend for help, but unfortunately your friend is unbelievably squeamish. Action!'

Real and Imaginary Ailments

One person asks 'Hello, how are you?' Instead of just replying 'Very well, thank you' or 'Not too bad', the other launches into a complete description of his or her medical condition. The twist is that they may either be describing the ailments they really have, or have recently had, or else they may be wholly imaginary ailments, and the rest of the group have to guess which. A good test of believability.

Suspicion

'If you've ever read Shakespeare's *Othello* you'll have been frustrated by all the unnecessary suspicion – through lack of trust. We, the audience, know what's going on but the characters don't – that's what's known as "dramatic irony".

'It's dreadful when someone feels betrayed. One of you feels very suspicious of the other's behaviour – nothing concrete, nothing you can quite put your finger on, but none the less your suspicions are aroused, especially since a mutual friend whispered something in your ear recently. First line – "What was that remark you made to Sandra on Friday?" Action!'

Marriage Scenes

A lot of duologues can be built round the lives of marriage partners or other couples who live together. Here are some examples:

> Breakfast time on the first day back at work after the honeymoon.
> She tells him she's going to have a baby.
> He comes home to tell her he's been made redundant.
> She's cooked his favourite dinner.
> He's cooked her favourite dinner.
> She hasn't cooked his dinner.
> He's been out late at the pub.
> She shouted at him that morning because the kids were under her feet. He's had a terrible day and is home late.
> He or she is having an affair and doesn't know if the other one suspects. The other doesn't.
> He or she is having an affair and this time the other one does suspect.
> They might have the mother of one of them living with them.

The Head

'The head' is an exercise in which each participant talks to an imaginary person represented by a head. Simply stand a wig block at head height on a plinth and give each participant a first line to start off in conversation with the head. The pieces are usually approximately a minute in length, but you can always put in the 'ten seconds to finish' signal from the sidelines. Remember, as well as talking to the head, each participant must listen, and react, to it as well.

First Lines

The first line provides an immediate way into a piece. The more open-ended the first line is, the better; and of course, you can sometimes make it optional. Here are some that have worked well for us:

'Promise you won't tell anyone.'
'Right! I've caught you now.'
'I've got an apology to make.'
'Please don't do that to me.'
'I've got a dreadful pain in my stomach.'
'Excuse me, I hope you don't think I'm being nosey.'
'I don't expect you had much chance to meet girls when you
     were at boarding school . . .'
'Trust you to spoil everything!'
'Is it the measles?'
'Look, snap out of it!'
'I don't believe it.'
'I beg your pardon.'
'It's disgusting!'
'Will you lend me . . .?'
'Don't you dare bring my mother into this!'
'Guess what happened to Mandy.'
'Chicken!'
'I'll give you three guesses what happened.'
'I've just lost Mum's purse.'
'What has your mum got against me?'
'I've told you before – the answer is *no*.'
'Stop that at once!'
'Johnny's been fired – did you know?'
'Can you keep a secret?'
'Don't you ever bring up that subject again!'
'Would you mind repeating that remark?'
'What on earth is the matter with you today?'
'Why can't you be punctual just for once?'
'Don't bite the hand that feeds you.'
'Why are you always picking on me?'
'What are you? A man or a mouse?'

'Money, money, money . . .'
'It's just not fair!'
'Why don't you ever listen to me?'
'My dog's just died . . .'
'What's the big idea, then?'
'Go on! Amaze me . . .'
'You've been talking about me behind my back, haven't you?'
'I saw you hit my little brother.'
'Don't go on and on and on about it.'
'Please don't tell her I told you.'
'What ever possessed you to do it?'
'You jealous or something?'
'He's/She's packed me in.'
'Why do you tell so many lies?'
'That's an excellent piece of work, but there's just one
    thing . . .'
'You've been chosen for a mission from which you are very
    unlikely to return . . .'
'I don't want to go to school today.'
'How can I tell him/her that it's over?'
'Do you know something? You really get up my nose.'
'Why are you always in such a bad temper?'
'Why did you tell Mum on me?'
'Dad's mad with you.'
'Don't be such a greedy-guts.'
'Stop pretending to be something you are not!'
'Don't be a dog in the manger!'
'Why can't you ever see it from my point of view?'
'Why did you hurt Mum's feelings like that?'
'You've got things out of all proportion.'
'Mum said, "Never accept lifts from strangers."'
'What a waste of money!'
'How dare you treat your pet like that?'
'I told you before, you must *not* bunk off school.'
'You're all mouth and no trousers.'
'It's easy to be an armchair critic – don't just sit there, *do*
    something.'
'Why do you give up so easily?'
'Why can't you take any criticism?'
'Haven't you got any manners?'
'Get up out of that bed immediately!'
'If you don't mind me saying so, you need to go on a diet.'

'I hate to say this, but I think you've got anorexia nervosa.'
'Look, I'm only giving you a warning.'
'Haven't you got any ambition in life?'
'Let them talk – who cares?'
'Shouting about it won't help.'
'This is absolutely the last straw.'
'You are so gullible.'
'I'm going to give you a piece of my mind.'
'You're getting a bit above yourself.'
'You haven't been very discreet, have you?'
'What do you mean by that sexist rubbish?'
'You're always making excuses! What is it this time?'
'Mum, I want to go abroad this year.'
'You really are very, very selfish.'
Scream! followed by 'You frightened the living daylights out
    of me.'
'I've had it up to here with you.'
'Grow up, will you? Act your age!'
'You're not old enough.'
'You are under my authority until you are eighteen.'
'You don't own me.'
'I'm sick to death of your prejudiced remarks.'
'Thanks for ruining my reputation.'
'You've let the cat out of the bag – that was supposed to be
    top secret.'
'Don't be a Scrooge.'
'Why are you always so nasty? Why can't you ever be nice?'
'Sarcasm is the lowest form of wit, didn't you know?'
'Look, Miss, you've got a grudge against me, haven't you?'
'What am I going to do? I'm heavily in debt.'
'Mum/Dad, can I have some more pocket money?' (Second
    line: 'More?')
'You're going to ruin your health.'
'I am not going to Nan's eightieth birthday.'
'Mum, I'm not coming home for Christmas this year.'
'You don't appreciate a thing I do.'
'No foul language in this house!'
'Sorry's just a word.'
'Don't be so pessimistic – look on the bright side.'
'Good grief! How petty can you be?'
'But, please, Mum . . .' (persuasion against will)
'How can you be so deceitful?'

'I feel sorry for you.'
'Look, I've got to get something off my chest.'

First lines can be used to start off monologues, duologues, soliloquies, or improvised plays. Sometimes you can give both the first and the second line, or even the second line only – in which case participants have a free choice of first line as long as it fits with the second. Try this with the second line 'You've just let the cat out of the bag.'

TECHNIQUE

Tongue-Twisters

Tongue-twisters provide an ideal verbal warm-up (after a vigorous physical one), being an aid to concentration, projection and diction. Four repetitions is enough for the one-liners; two or three for the longer ones. Start by saying, 'After two. One, two ...'

Red leather, yellow leather

Red lolly, yellow lorry

Mixed biscuits

Unique New York

Richard gave Robin a rap in the ribs for roasting his rabbit so rare.

Sly Sam sips Sally's soup.

Betty bought a bit of butter,
But the butter Betty bought was bitter,
So Betty bought a better bit of butter
Than the butter Betty bought before.

Six sleek swans swam swiftly southwards.

If a gumboil could boil oil,
How much oil could a gumboil boil
If a gumboil could boil oil?

Three grey geese in a green field grazing,
Grey were the geese and green was the grazing.

How much wood would a woodchuck chuck
If a woodchuck could chuck wood?

Five flies flew round the farmyard
Frightening the farmer's friend.

Lazy Lenny licks Lucy's lolly.

Pack a copper kettle.

Round and round the rugged rocks
The ragged rascal ran.

Elly's elegant elephant

Harry from Hampstead hangs his hat on a hanger,
Hannah hangs hers on a hook in the hall.

If a good cook could cook cuckoos
How many cuckoos could a good cook cook
If a good cook could cook cuckoos?

Three fiddling pigs sit in a pit and fiddle,
Fiddle piggy, fiddle piggy, fiddle piggy.

A pleasant place to place a plaice
Is a place where a plaice
Is pleased to be placed.

I can think of thin things,
Six thin things, can you?
Yes I can think of six thin things
And of six thick things too.

Selfish shellfish.

Double bubble gum bubbles double.

Bed spreaders spread beds.
But bread spreaders spread bread.

Good blood, bad blood.

Can you imagine an imaginary menagerie manager
Imagining managing an imaginary menagerie?

Really rural.

This thistle seems like that thistle.

Sally's selfish selling shellfish
So Sally's shellfish seldom sell.

The sun shines on shop signs.

Which is the witch that wished the wicked wish?

Miss Smith dismisseth us.

Silver thimbles.

Peggy Babcock.

Tuesday is stewday, stewday is Tuesday.

For sheep soup — shoot sheep.

Super thick sticky tape.

This slim spider slid slowly sideways.

If you notice this notice you'll notice this notice is not worth noticing.

Pink pomegranate, purple pomegranate.

Once you start collecting tongue twisters your list will grow and grow. Once word gets round, the children will be forever adding to it. But, as with all ideas, do keep a record.

Stage Presence

Some people talk about stage presence as if it is a gift that one either does or does not have. Although some people do indisputably have it naturally, it is possible for anyone to improve their stage presence by developing their technique. What people need to do is to overcome and disguise their natural feelings of shyness. Some of the secrets of stage presence are:

Stillness   Avoiding body fidgeting, small hand and head movements, face-touching.

Energy   Both in movement and use of the voice. Fitness is the key to this.

Controlled Aggression   To be successful any performer must be prepared to give it everything and 'go for it'.

Crispness of Persona
Eye Contact
Total Concentration

The following exercises can be used to develop these aspects of stage presence.

Eye Contact   A group of people stroll down a beach and each of them fixes his eyes on something that interests him in the water. The 'something' is in the same position as the eyes of someone in the audience.

Dominance   Two science-fiction creatures confront each other. After a while one prevails and the other backs down without a fight. Freeze in the positions of dominance and submission.

Mastermind Plus   The 'victims' are spotlit in a chair and are grilled with harder and harder questions. If they don't know the answers they are made to work them out. Through all this they have to maintain a calm appearance. They are 'out' if they touch their face, fidget their hands, body or feet, shrug or laugh.

Energy Contest   Two people try to race each other round parallel courses of equal length. Anyone giving maximum energy, win or lose, passes the test and is allowed to have a rest. Those who fail have to race again against someone else.

Addressing the Rally   On the eve of an election, a political candidate in a country where democracy is threatened addresses a rally in a football stadium. He must make a final emotional appeal to the people to save the country. He must offer the last drop of his blood to them and give them a vision of the future they can still have. Nothing less than total commitment will be enough.

Script-Reading

If you're doing mainly improvisation-based drama, it makes a change occasionally to do script-reading. Apart from being practice at the generally useful skill of reading at sight, it is a good way of extending your students' knowledge of plays.

In any typical group of youngsters, you will find many who are either dyslexic or else poor sight-readers for one reason or another. Often the memory of past humiliations will add to their nervousness and make things worse. It is worth reassuring them that many people have reading difficulties – for example, the actress Susan Hampshire – and it is best to start with something as easy to read as you can find. If possible give them some time to read over and prepare what they are going to do. One useful tip is to encourage them to read at a slow pace; not only will this help them read more accurately, but it will also help them to read with good expression and intonation. Encourage them to read with natural pauses and not at one pace like a dictation exercise. Tell them to 'read the punctuation': a comma is a short pause, a full stop a longer one. Believability is still essential; they must imagine themselves right inside the part, even though they are reading it off the page. If someone makes a mistake, the natural tendency is to hurry up, as if to make up for lost time, and this often leads to more mistakes, so a good piece of advice is: 'If you make a mistake, slow down.'

VIDEO WORK

Many schools and clubs now have access to video equipment, so here are some suggestions for effective ways of using it. The first problem to overcome is the embarrassment barrier of seeing and hearing oneself on the screen for the first time. Everyone, particularly adolescents, seems to find that no one else looks and sounds as peculiar as they do. Anything that makes people self-conscious in their acting is not going to be helpful, so it is a good idea to start with students who are already well used to improvising and to have a first familiarization session purely so that they can be in front of the camera and see what they look and sound like on the screen.

Recording a lesson as it happens and then pointing out things and commenting on playback is a useful way of using video as a general teaching tool. Remember that playback takes just as long as recording, so if you are going to record a whole session and then watch it that will halve the amount of time you can use on the session. Then you can start to work on some of the elements of screen acting. The audience sees the actors from much nearer, particularly in close-up, so all effects are magnified and it is necessary to underplay relative to what one would do with a theatre audience. The actor must avoid exaggerated facial expressions and sudden movements that would take him out of camera shot. Talking to camera, a television technique, requires the subject to look directly at the lens and speak to it, imagining it to be a person he or she is talking to. Any look away from camera needs to be positive or it will look oddly surreptitious.

Video opens out possibilities of exploring subtlety in performances, particularly in work involving emotional reactions where you can use the direction 'The emotion is still there, but the character's not showing it.' It is particularly useful for character work and ideas such as the 'in-depth interview', which, being an imaginary television interview, works every bit as well when videoed, whether in preparation for a production or not.

If you do a production, it is nice to have a video recording as a permanent record. Doing this at a dress rehearsal rather than at a performance gives you more freedom of choice of camera positions, and also gives you the option of rerunning a scene if necessary. The next step is to mount your own video productions and, depending on the technical resources you have available, the sky's the limit.